PEACE @ ENOUGH

Peace Comes With Satisfaction; Satisfaction Comes With Achievement of Enough; Enough Can Vary Individually.

AF121031

DHRUV GUPTA

BLUEROSE PUBLISHERS
India | U.K.

Copyright © Dhruv Gupta 2023

All rights reserved by author. No part of this publication may be reproduced, stored in a retrieval system or transmitted in any form or by any means, electronic, mechanical, photocopying, recording or otherwise, without the prior permission of the author. Although every precaution has been taken to verify the accuracy of the information contained herein, the publisher assume no responsibility for any errors or omissions. No liability is assumed for damages that may result from the use of information contained within.

BlueRose Publishers takes no responsibility for any damages, losses, or liabilities that may arise from the use or misuse of the information, products, or services provided in this publication.

For permissions requests or inquiries regarding this publication, please contact:

BLUEROSE PUBLISHERS
www.BlueRoseONE.com
info@bluerosepublishers.com
+91 8882 898 898
+4407342408967

ISBN: 978-93-5819-503-3

Cover design: Muskan Sachdeva
Typesetting: Pooja Sharma

First Edition: July 2023

श्री गणेशाय नमः

वक्रतुण्ड महाकाय सूर्यकोटि समप्रभ।
निर्विघ्नं कुरु मे देव सर्वकार्येषु सर्वदा॥

श्री हनुमान जी सदा सहाय

Peace Comes with Satisfaction; Satisfaction Comes with Achievement of Enough; Enough Can Vary Individually

This book is dedicated to:

All well-wishers, without whom life would not have been as exciting, challenging, and enlightening as it is today.

Look around; so many well-wishers contribute like signposts on this journey called life. Mentioning a few names would be an injustice to others. It's such a long list of beautiful, compassionate people that a separate book will be required to detail how they came to help even without asking for it.

There are givers, there are takers, and there are equalizers. It is bliss, and maybe the outcome of my past karmas, that so many givers came across to support me in dire need. Life is all about interdependence; there is not a single event or phenomenon that is independent. Givers very well balance the ecosystem of this interdependence by continuing to give without expecting reciprocation. Taking is not a sin unless 'one is only a taker." It is so important to give back to society to keep the balance in this realm of interdependence.

But I must give credit to one person, Monica, who knows all my weaknesses yet keeps me motivated and cheers throughout. Life does not seem possible without her—my wife, soul mate, and mentor. She, along with my daughter, Dr. Abhaya, son, Sidhant, always stand shoulder to shoulder by my side, thick and thin. We called ourselves 'Super 4."

On February 2023, our family welcomed Sumit Ji, a caring, sharp observer, and clear-thinking son-in-law. Now we are 'Super 5," bolder than before and happier than before.

I must also mention my gratitude to all the players in the stories and, most importantly, the narrator of these backstories.

These backstories span about a century, from the 1920s. Any resemblance may be just a coincidence and be ignored. Historical references that are relevant to these stories have been picked up from the internet and are alluded to simply to depict the chronology, the time, the period, and the environment. One must validate them if required before sharing or forming an opinion about these historical references.

Foreword

We have 7,922,312,800, or roughly 8 billion players with their life stories today on Earth. Every minute, 140 new life stories are born, while every minute, 106 life stories are ending. (World Population Review.com and Medindia's World Death Calculator) The earth is full of success stories and failure stories.

Each player has a life journey on Earth with its own peculiar challenges, twists and turns, highs and lows, happy and tough times, successes and failures.

This book captures a few of these life stories and their quest for peace. The quest for life and a peaceful life have always been the same, while the time, period, environment, and place may be different. It transcends time. The basic needs across the globe are common, and thus the response to achieve these, being the basic needs of survival, also transcends time.

This book shall resonate with readers of all age groups, allowing them to derive their own takeaway as per their socio-economic status. For the reader's clarity of the socio-economic environment, the book beautifully captures the relatable events of the period to give a simple background for easy comprehension.

The writing style is engaging and accessible, making it easy for readers to follow along and connect with the book's message. It offers a fresh perspective on personal fulfilment, encouraging readers to prioritize their well-being and inner peace over external validation and endless pursuits. It serves as a reminder that true contentment lies in finding "enough" within ourselves.

These backstories are still relevant; therefore, this book has the potential to transcend time.

However, challenges for players in the future might be different from today. 50 years down the line, life's quest may be to be able to differentiate between the virtual world and the real world, how to avoid virtual living or how much of virtual living shall be enough, how to get to the real world, how to differentiate between robotic emotions and human emotions, how to establish deep personal contact between humans, and how to define actual peace vs. virtual peace. The virtual world shall be like a person in a coma, and the challenge would be to come out of the coma into the actual world. A conflict between the virtual and real worlds

The player's quest, however, shall remain the same to achieve peace, and they shall still have to determine their Enough in the context prevailing at that time, period, and environment.

This book provides a thought-provoking exploration of peace and satisfaction through relatable anecdotes, philosophical reflections, and practical insights reflected through stories spanning over a century.

The message resonates with readers seeking a more peaceful and satisfying life by encouraging them to manage expectations from themselves and others; to define what is "enough" at different stages of life; to adapt one's goals and expectations to the current context; and to be realistic and adaptable in their pursuit of peace and satisfaction.

The author's emphasis on managing stress, nurturing faith, and acknowledging unexpected help resonates with readers seeking strategies to cope with life's challenges. By incorporating these elements, the author encourages readers to develop resilience and a positive mindset, ultimately leading to a more peaceful and satisfying life.

Start a journey towards inner satisfaction and peace. Enjoy reading this book and, having liked it, recommend it to family and friends.

The Ghost Writer

Contents

Introduction 1

The Narrator... 7

The Awakening Decade- Roaring Twenties............ 13

The Childhood 20

The Astrologer, Mining Engineer & a Journalist... 32

The Love, Marriage & the Wait............................ 41

The Knowledge & Efforts Never Go Waste........... 50

The Wife & the Mother 56

A Gold That Didn't Glitter 64

She the Hustler 76

The Beauty Parlour 90

Ainth (ਐਠ) - Not Less Than Any............................ 99

The Unwilling Salesman....................................... 107

Conclusion: Peace @ Enough 125

Gratitude 131

Introduction

Humans, at all points in life, yearn for peace and desire it. This yearning or desire transcends time, is omnipresent, has always been there, and shall always be, irrespective of time, period, or environment. Since ages, a lot has been written about what peace is and how to attain it. These works have been written by proven authorities on such subjects. But rest assured, no work on this subject will be the last.

"Contemporary lifestyle demands" create a lot of unproductive stress. Productive stress leads to positive outcomes, while unproductive stress leads to fear, frustration, and dissatisfaction. It creates a haze that prevents clarity and does not allow clear thinking.

The light of faith and trust leads to clear thinking and removes unproductive stress, fears of failure, and frustration, thereby fostering confidence and smiles. 'Unexpected Help' arrives. Just take a moment to remember an "unexpected help" that came to you when it was badly needed, no matter how small the matter. Make a mental album or repository of positive nostalgia for all such "unexpected help," keep adding to it, and refer to it to realize how blissful life is. There's some "unexpected help" on the way when it is needed the most. It is not merely positive thinking but experience-based trust stemming from "unexpected help" that has been received based on true-life events. Positive nostalgia always reduces stress and infuses happiness. Close the doors to unproductive stress with faith and trust.

Another common source of unproductive stress is "over expectation." Our own expectations of ourselves and others; others' expectations of us, etc. Just as we manage all things in life, "expectation" management is also a must. What is the desired achievement level? Does it fall within a person's scope or the time at hand? How much is the right achievement level?

Life is a progression, and therefore, achievement levels have to also be a progressive complement to time, period, and environment. The best way to manage "expectation," or rather, the achievement level, is by understanding and deciding what is "enough" at that time. The definition of "enough" is dynamic and paced progressively with life.

One of the ways to define "enough" is reflected in Sant Kabir's following saying:

"Sai Itna Dijiye, Jaa Me Kutum Samay

Mai Bhi Bhukha Na Rahu, Sadhu Bhi Bhukha Na Jaye."

Sant Kabir is praying to God to provide enough so that his family, who is dependent on him, can live without going hungry, and neither he nor any person visiting his house is required to go back with an empty stomach.

There is a proverb: "If wishes were horses, beggars would ride." It was first recorded about 1628 in a collection of Scottish proverbs. It implies that if simply wishing could make things happen, then even the most destitute people would have everything they wanted. There would be no pain, no poverty, and nothing remaining to wish for because one would get everything one wished for. But in the real world, this is not the case.

Making a wish, setting up a goal or target, and defining "enough" are all different. When making a wish, even the sky is not the limit; one can wish for anything one can think of. To simplify understanding, let's say a goal or target is composed of possible wishes, which may or may not be fully achieved. Even if 99% of the goal or target is achieved, the remaining 1% will always pinch. "Enough" is a position in which even if the goal or target is not achieved, it is still sufficient to move on and survive; loosely, it can be called financial freedom.

Defining "enough" does not mean defining short- or long-term goals. It means defining actions and achievements to reach these short- or long-term goals. It, in no way, means restricting efforts, lowering enthusiasm, or diminishing ambitions. It encompasses Josh (enthusiasm), Soch (ambition), and Hosh (defining ENOUGH)—managing expectations.

"Enough" does not lead to inaction; it is the optimization of achievements with maximum efforts within the scope and given time, period, and environment. Time, period, and environment are extremely important factors to consider in defining "enough." Thus, "enough" during COVID has to be different than in the post-COVID time, period, and environment. Could it be the same?

What is 'ENOUGH' for one person may not be 'ENOUGH' for another.

Needless to say, with trust and faith in "unexpected help" and a defined "enough," life can progress without unproductive stress, with a lot of enjoyable moments leading to "peace at enough."

The PEACE @ ENOUGH is a stress-free lifestyle concept. There are no sermons in this short book; there are no prescribed methods or formulas for peace or exercises at the end of each story. It contains life stories that clearly reflect that peace is possible. No effort has been made to highlight the 'moral of the story," and it is up to the esteemed readers to derive their takeaways. This book has been kept short to hold the reader's attention since the span of attention is getting shorter with every passing day.

Most of the time, a mental album of "unexpected help" automatically gets created. These have made me resilient enough to keep up with the odds and sail through.

At the age of 55 plus, I can vividly see through the events and "unexpected help" that have come my way. In fact, it was only about a year ago or so that I started linking current support with past actions—people known and unknown, extending a helping hand as "unexpected help."

The stories, however, are not about my experiences with "unexpected help" and defining "enough." The backstories span around a century, with references from pre-independence to the present. These players have been introduced to me by the narrator through their backstories. These players have been given different names, and their whereabouts have also not been stated in the stories. This has been done to safeguard their privacy. An element of fiction has been added to real events to build the fabric of the stories. Efforts have been made to ensure that the backstories do not become relatable to any person, living or dead. However, if that happens, it is inadvertent, not intended, and should be overlooked.

Go ahead and enjoy reading the PEACE @ ENOUGH simple backstories without putting any pressure on your mind, body, or soul to learn anything from them. The mind retains what it must and reproduces it when it is needed most.

Stay happy and healthy in life, always.

God bless.

The Narrator

PEACE @ ENOUGH is not about my life's confluences with PEACE. It is about Player's introduced to me by The Narrator. There are NPCs – (non-playing characters) but stories are pivoted to Players.

Most of us born in 50s, 60s & 70s, have grown listening to stories from our mother, aunts viz Bua ji & Tai ji, Daadi - Daada ji, and other elders of house. Families used to be mostly joint which meant about 20 to 25 people under one roof or even more. These stories played crucial part in forming character, morality and conduct. Each story had a moral which was well narrated making it easy to understand. I have not read our great epics but know almost all major events/descriptions thru story telling alongside logical explanations & beliefs. The narratives were built with the common objective of making the child a good human being, God-fearing, developing good habits & ability to differentiate good & bad, sense of responsibility & strong belief in faith & karma. We as children/ listeners, believed since these stories were told by our loved ones whom we trusted blindly.

Stories have always been a powerful tool for ages to convey a message. They leave a long-lasting impression in the mind because a child/ listener always has full faith and complete belief in the story teller. These stories help create a narrative that impacts the mind even without having to know or check facts. Every day, we see narratives being created thru stories in our socio-political circles and we form our belief basis these narratives, what matters is how much we trust the story teller. The Realities are distant and unseen, but their narrative is seen. Faith in the narrator leads one to believe these, and from opinions & actions.

The truth can be different to different people. Therefore, it is important to be impartial in our minds and to be able to see the truth without any perceptions. The narratives are not impartial, these are created to confuse if not convince, and to get away with one's ideology, deeds & actions. One can have an impartial mind if one is focused on 'Objective' and evaluates what is directed to achieving objective. Objective has to be noble, in interests of society, human race and not harmful to any entity. It is simple, the way you validate credentials of a person then you allow entry, give your trust, access to emotions and mind space after validating the real agenda/objective of any narrative.

Be dynamic in taking U-turn the moment you get to know of the ulterior motive of the narratives.

It is my trust in the Narrator that these backstories are being shared here to showcase examples of ordinary people who have embraced peace. Peace Seeking is a continuous process and not a one-time action. It is at every twist & turn of life that we need to build Peace around us with our thoughts and actions. It is interesting to know how Players define what is 'Enough' at each stage for them to achieve it and move on to achieve next 'Enough'. Also, they got so many Unexpected Helps which came unexpectedly but their seeds got planted/sowed prior.

Typically, we hear tales of famous people who, despite clear life odds, rose to prominence or fortune through pure effort and resolve. It goes without saying that chance/luck always has a significant impact. They are undoubtedly shining examples in and of themselves, however, how many everyday individuals who bravely confront such challenges & triumph but gain popularity? That's why I chose to share these back stories of 'next door ordinary Players' who have faced challenges as we all do and took certain steps to come out shining & happy. Look around & you would find so many inspiring stories in your own social circle. Why look for handful of famous to get motivation. It can be even your story thus far to keep pushing you for continuous hustling. Positive Nostalgia is very important to keep pedaling.

The Narrator & I know each other for a long now; but how close we know each other is yet to be understood! Sometimes, I feel I know him to the extent I know myself but other times I feel I am yet to know him well enough. Whenever we find time to be alone & together, away from the daily grind, he shares back stories of players who thru their modesty, willpower, hard work, grit, resilience, honest approach, straightforwardness, keeping things simple and managing expectations have cultivated Peace & happiness. The smiles on their faces reflect contentment & PEACE. Their lives are /have not been picture perfect, faced more failures probably, and they have faced lows & highs of life. These Players have never shot to fame. They are/ have lived 'life ordinary' like millions of us. Somehow, nobody talks or writes about such successes around us. If one looks around, every life has a success story to talk about. Reading here about these Players may prompt you to look around & find winners all around with smiles, content & PEACE.

The Narrator wished to be anonymous & not relate himself with these players /stories. Strange though because this is the World of likes & Shares. The moment some matter is posted on social media everyone gets eager to see popularity. But here I have this person who did not wish to be named! I have never felt anything lacking in his life, he seems to have enough. Again, not a famous person, ordinary next-door types, no hype no showoffs nothing. Mostly with a sincere smile when talking. Do I feel good in his company? Yes. It was he who always connected by unexpectedly walking in. He lived a life away from technology no mobile and no social media. He practiced deep personal interaction rather than using digital mediums to connect. Deep personal interactions always leave long-lasting impacts, and happy memories & stimulate positivity.

After the first wave of Covid19, I did ask him to write short stories about people he knew but he refused and laughingly asked me to write if I wished. Then came the delta variant which created havoc. Actually, I had to delete close to 15 contacts from my phone book who could not win over the delta variant. He has not connected with me since. I wish him well and hope someday he shall walk in unexpectedly with that ingenuous smile and a beaming face for another memorable deep personal interaction.

PEACE @ ENOUGH is neither about The Narrator's life. The back stories are spanning for around 100 years, some are living and some are gone. Journey from small town to big city, from small canvas to bigger canvas with limited means & lot of hard toil, joyful moments and failures are all part of these lives. As promised, there shall be no sermons, no take away, no exercise, no principals told. These are back stories of simple people who strived PEACE @ ENOUGH and are not/have not become famous public figures, yet contended & happy. Visualize these stories without straining your mind, body & soul. It is said 'it takes a lifetime to learn' probably these life stories may have some learnings which could benefit.

It is likely that some events depicted in these stories may be relatable and you, yourself may become the Player for a while. Go on draw your own take away & ways to PEACE @ ENOUGH.

ENOUGH shall be different for different people, it would be different at different times, and each situation can have its 'ENOUGH'. ENOUGH has no greed. Greed can never be part of 'ENOUGH', if it is then what you desire is not actually 'ENOUGH'...greed is never-ending race. Also, there are no comparisons to be made while defining what 'ENOUGH' is. The limit of social comparison is so high that virtually no one can ever reach it which means that it's a quest that can never be achieved & best way to reach the limit is to accept that you may have less than others but what you have is ENOUGH for you. Thus, define your ENOUGH.

Go on & find your PEACE @ ENOUGH.

The Awakening Decade- Roaring Twenties

Stories are abounding; thus, a beginning must be chosen out of entire bouquet of back stories. Let's begin with the period of 1920s. Stories spanning over a Century with two generations are being picked up. Quest remains same for survival & growth.

The decade seeded contemporary advancement. While West had proceeded on advancement, Indians decided to be Free from British Raj. Their ENOUGH was the Freedom & own rule. They did not wish to be left behind for becoming a developing Nation.

The 1920s decade was marked with changes around the World. It was a period of new learnings, growth, exploration & trend setting.

America gained status of World Power post WW I, as it was no longer recognized as British Colony with decline of Europe. This period was called Roaring Twenties in the US, Europe termed it as Golden Twenties due to economic boom post WW I.

The era saw the large-scale adoption of automobiles, telephones, motion pictures, radio and household electricity, as well as unprecedented industrial growth, accelerated consumer demand and aspirations, and significant changes in lifestyle and culture. The media began to focus on celebrities, especially sports heroes and movie stars.

Major developments around Globe included voting right for Women starting from the UK, US and other Nations including Madras province in British India. Rise of Communism political movement led by USSR- Soviet Union & Fascism led by Italy. League of Nations & other associated bodies were formed to avoid wars & for international cooperation. The Great Depression Oct 1929 ended economic boom which started post WW I.

This decade saw a host of Science & Technology advancements, to mention a few:

The development of the first color television and the first functional mechanical television system led to the first all-talking film, the first all-color all-talking film, and the first film featuring a soundtrack. Commercial manufacture of CRT tubes, which are used in computers and televisions. Phonograph records are first recorded using an electrical technique. Patents for the first electric razor and a frozen food preparation method were also filed. The first liquid-fueled rocket launch. The creation of penicillin. Mickey Mouse appears in Walt Disney's debut animated short film, which was released in 1928. The first animated film with sound was Steamboat Willie. India was also undergoing change. India, under the British Raj, was a founding member of the League of Nations, a participating member in the Olympics, and a founding member of the United Nations. This was the decade in which the seeds were sown for complete independence.

This was the Time of awareness, unity & social changes; A Period when Britain weakened post WWI and An Environment full of patriotism, the Free India dream.

The freedom movement was gaining momentum & support from common people. Gandhi Ji entered in India freedom movement scene. He travelled the length & breadth of India to understand its nuances. Neta ji also came back to India after studying abroad on patriotism calling & became a member of INC and later became INC president as well.

India launched the Non-Cooperation Movement with Gandhi Ji steering it. It stemmed due to the outrage following the Jallianwala Bagh massacre in Amritsar when British-led troops gunned down nearly 400 unarmed residents and injured several of them. The victims were merely celebrating Baisakhi in the Bagh and peacefully protesting the arrest of two Indian leaders. The Non-cooperation Movement is believed to be the first national-level protest in India's freedom struggle. This decade saw Chouri Chaura, Demand for Purna Swaraj – Complete Independence; Bardoli Satyagrah; Civil Disobedience & Salt Movement to name major movements.

This was the decade which saw the beginning of Hindu-centric organization/s with the sole purpose of uniting otherwise divided & weakened Hindus to strengthen the Hindu majority community, propagate Hindu ideology & create a Hindu nationalist movement. The harmony can be achieved by creating a balanced equilibrium of ideological power, muscle power, strength & fear.

Harmony can never be there in an expansionist environment. Harmony does not exist between a weak & a strong. The human race is known as the psyche of superiority since time immemorial. Therefore, we are watching a race of acquiring more & more weapons of mass destruction, some nations using these as deterrents & some for their expansionism and race to superiority. Usage as a deterrent is creating harmony & fearfulness.

This was the period when patriotism was peaking for Complete Independence. There shall hardly be any soul in India which may not have wished for Freedom. At the political echelons, the dream of heading Government started seeding and Gandhi ji was destined to have a major role to play.

This was the decade where in popular Bollywood & Film personalities were born- Dev Anand & Pran, Sahir Ludhianvi, Satyajit Ray, Dilip Kumar, Dina Pathak, Ajit Khan, Mrinal Sen, Johnny Walker, N. T. Rama Rao, Mukesh, Raj Kapoor, Mohammed Rafi, Pradeep Kumar, Guru Dutt, Sunil Dutt, Raaj Kumar, Uttam Kumar, Prem Nath, Kishore Kumar, Lata Mangeshkar, Yash Johar, Utpal Dutt, Nargis & many more legendry singers, writers, directors and actors.

This was the decade in which many political leaders were born like Atal Bihari Bajpayee, Narsimha Rao, N T Ramarao, Chandrashekar, Lal Krishna Advani etc. this decade was the growing up period of Indira Gandhi.

Did anyone know that these personalities born in this decade would shape the future of Free India on Politics, Art, Culture & Socio-Economic fronts?

The State (now it's a city) was under Nawab rule and leaned towards British Raj, therefore, had more of a peaceful life with not much adverse impact from the

British Empire. In the State treasury, worked a Lala who had two sons – one became a saint at an adolescent age and the other was groomed into a Money Lender. It was a period of high mortality rate & life expectancy was somewhere between 21 to 25 years only. This led to having many children, the joint family was a social norm. Most of families thus had 7 to 8 siblings & being a joint family of around 20 – 25 people which kind of necessitated a big house if one could afford it. Early marriages & early children were social norm. Most of the time, there would be 4 births taking place around the same time in a family or a house- Mother, Daughter in law/s, Daughter and to avoid an inauspicious figure 3 an expecting Cow was kept till all the deliveries including Cow happened. ☺ It was not a coincident that youngest uncle - Chacha ji or aunt- Bua ji & eldest nephew/niece were either same age or had small age gap & grew together.

Money lending business was a form of banking to simplify but with rules set by money lenders basis the power they could wield; totally unorganized business, unregulated thus there were good ones & bad ones. Watch 'Mother India' a 1957 Bollywood movie with Sunil Dutt and Nargis starred to know how money landers could be a parasite & cruel. This was the last movie on this subject if my memory is correct. Good ones were without greed & cruelty and carried it as a pure business, bad ones were with greed & cruelty. But both had to keep muscular & tough-looking recovery persons.

It was a vicious circle for borrowers extending to the next generations at times. All this was because borrowers were mostly illiterates and could not keep tabs on interests & principal being repaid, rulers did not lend money in an organized form they however collected taxes to run their Kingdoms/States.

As a, guarantee borrowers pledged their homes, fields, gold jewelry even farm and working animals. Failure to repay in time would mean loss of ownership by borrowers in favor of money lender or extension with a penalty.

Money Lender had thus seven surviving children, 4 sons and 3 daughters. Money was not an issue at all. They all were quite handsome and fair, their daughters were good features, fair & beautiful. Each was destined to their own tortuous life filled with struggles, failures & successes.

The Narrator shared back stories of the second son. Since stories were verbal, there are fair chances of some differences in interpretations of events.

The Childhood

The Players share common upbringing, socio economic geography, political & educational environment thus had equal or same opportunities/upbringing yet their lives unfolded quite differently. Infused with same values yet they grew to be different, different beliefs, different values & different understanding of life. This clearly reflect that surroundings, environment & people around have astounding impact on the person one become.

"If a drop of water falls on a hot pan, it gets erased. If it falls on a lotus leaf, it starts shining like a pearl. And if it falls into an oyster, it itself becomes a pearl. A drop of water is the same, only the company is different". – Unknown.

There is an English proverb 'A man is known by the company he keeps' This expression is derived from a fable written by Aesop in the 500s B.C called "The Ass and his Purchaser". In the story, a man takes an ass to his farm on a trial basis to see how the ass will fit into his herd of asses. When the ass enters the pasture, he seeks out the laziest and greediest ass that the man owns to keep company. The man returns the ass because he knows it too will be lazy and greedy, based on the animal the ass chose to spend time with. The moral of the story in short is that a man is known by the company he keeps.

The Player's life has been tortuous but there are a lot of common characteristics they exhibited like hard work, always believe in action, acquiring knowledge & skills, resilience, good sense of humor, modesty, helping attitude, kind-hearted, straightforwardness, caring, self-respect, challenge readiness, stress resilience, will power & faith in Supreme to name a few here. They trusted what their parents said about challenges & future & I believe most of us trust them for their guidance and advice, especially in adversities.

Their journey started in the small city situated in the terai region of the Himalayas. As per medieval history, the city was ruled by Katheria Rajputs who fought for 400 years the sultans of Delhi & later with Moguls. The Rohilla State was established by Nawab Faizullah Khan on 7 October 1774 in the presence of British Commander Colonel Champion, and remained a pliant state under British.

About 5 decades ago, the mountain range was easily visible from this city during any weather. Even now after excessive rains when pollution levels fall, this mountain range becomes visible. Ancient habitats were mostly situated near rivers and so does this city alongside river Kosila, the Himalayan River originating from Uttarakhand having 168 Km length having farms & temples alongside. Millets, which current leadership is promoting at the World Forum to alleviate hunger and promote health, is one of the major agricultural produce along with tomatoes and wheat as per respective seasons.

A picturesque city, with Palace domes, visible from far-off entry points to the city. A combination of Mogul & British architecture and a place in the history of India ruled by Nawabs till merged with the Union of India under drive of the Loh Purush in 1949.

Most of the cities in India are bifurcated into two – an old city & new generally called as civil lines. So, does this one. Purana bus adda (bus stand) & naya bus adda so on and so forth. The old city laid out with closely clustered houses called a mohalla with each one having a name. Postmen used to deliver letters not with house number but with name of the person and mohalla-locality. Pin code was also not much needed. Letters were sent thru postcards and inland letters. If some information was to be hidden then envelopes with tickets were used. If someone did not want the receiver to purchase a postcard to reply, there were 'reply paid post cards' just like prepaid service. ETA of letters used to be somewhere between 15 days to 30 days. For faster communication, there was the telegram which mostly brought bad news. Ladies used to start crying hearing that a telegram has come. Telephones were not in every home and outstation calls were made by booking a trunk call. Telephone operators used to call the person and once connected, call back to the caller and connect the line & entire conversation was being heard by the operator since they had to cut the line within the time limit set for call metering. Call Extension was allowed and 2nd call charge was levied. For urgent calls lightning call' option was there though expensive. Since Government was aware that every house does not have a phone and people allowed neighbors to use telephones. There was a mechanism called PP Call, which meant that call rates would not be assessed until the intended recipient arrived from the surrounding area and answered the call. In PP calls, the operator would leave a message asking the phone owner to call the neighbor back in ten minutes. People had no qualms about letting their neighbors use their amenities, including their televisions, which were first used in 1959 as an experiment before going nationwide in 1982. Till 1976 radio and television services were together. It was a license raj with Radio and TV both required to have a license to use which was to be renewed every year. Radio was more common than black & white TV and telephone, with more families having their own big one like an OTG size today. The First Radio private service started in 1927, AIR came into existence in 1937. We were not FREE then.

The old city house had more than 20 rooms three veranda, three courtyards originally built more than 200 years ago. The courtyards were in center of house facing them were veranda. Front of the house was for gents (Mardana) and back of the house meant for ladies (Ganana). Rooms were so interconnected that one could move in entire house without actually getting into day light. There was a well in back portion of the house alongside open kitchen system. Sewage system was all manual. Stairs to roof were small with only a person can either go up or come down. It was probably a part of house design those days. House had two separate entries. There was a basement called tehkhana to keep valuables below Vernanda in the Mardana section. It had a staircase covered with wooden flooring and a square opening for light and air to go in. The entire veranda used to be carpeted fully. This house was built by Lala and passed on to the next generation. The money lender lived here with a HUF, a joint family.

Schooling & most of college days were spent in a civil lines house which was referred to then as a bungalow. Single story with own driveway, two lawns, back courtyard, a farming land attached to something like what is known as Farm House today. Two bungalows were together with each having separate adjacent facilities except that drive way was common for both. This was a British-style house with then modern facilities like an independent sewage system, bedrooms drawing rooms, dining room, bathrooms, kitchen, Veranda & Chabootra- a raised platform beside Veranda. The veranda was on looking front lawn and Chabootra was on looking side lawn.

Nature was in abundance with lush green surroundings with Mango, Guava, Jamun & Grapes trees around. Vicinity gave enough space for snakes, mongooses, frogs, monkeys and colorful birds of all types. Street dogs and pets were always around. Thieves had a new trick up their sleeve, they trained dogs to open door latches for easy entry. One such dog came to stay but theft never took place. It was a dual-toned indie boy lovingly called 'Blacky'.

Radio, clubs, indoor and outdoor games including table tennis, badminton, carom, cricket, and football, as well as socializing with friends, going to fairs and melas, viewing Ram Leela, and attending other socio-religious events were the main sources of entertainment. The front and side lawns were utilized for football and cricket, respectively. Since there were two swings attached to the sturdy branches of a mango tree, they could be used year-round and continuously. The goal of the competition was to swing so high that your foot touched another branch. Oblivious of outcome of a fall, almost every day it was attempted by children. Ladies used to play cards together in neighborhood like kitty parties these days. The card game of Bridge & Chess, were status symbols & thus was learned by all ladies and gents. Flash (teen patti) along with Paplu called Indian Rummy was another time pass card games. For kids, there were many card games like teen-do-panch, saat-aath, kotpees etc. Ludo, Snakes & Ladder, chess, hide & seek etc. were all played regularly as a time pass.

The factory compound had an open-air theatre where every month a film was shown to all workers & staff. Wall was painted white and a projector was used to show the film. On festivals there were Ram Leela and open theatre conducted in that place.

The biggest entertainment was off-course Picture Halls or Cinema Ghar or Talkies as known in those days. There were no multiplexes as today. These were individual screen theaters. These movies lead the fashion even in small towns and cities. We talk of nightlife these days, while it was prevalent then also with night shows ending at about 12.30 – 01 AM. Then there were early morning shows starting from 4.00 AM. Actually, Cinema was almost 24X7. Timings for every customer, family, bachelors & all classes. Another entertainment was the club which used to be open till past midnight & it housed all indoor/outdoor games. Officers played cards normally it was a game of bridge with wins and lose noted for the final point tally. There was this annual Exhibition a big mela event on the outskirts of the city which used to start from 7.30 pm and go on till early morning. Night life concept is not recent, it prevailed then as well. Yes, talkies were bigger entertainers with many in a city. Commuting mostly was thru rickshaws which were available round the clock picking up passengers from rail stations, bus stations and cinema halls. Like Today, cabs operate 24X7, it was rickshaws which were there. Rickshaw walas worked in shifts. 24X7 life was on with factories & cinema running all shifts.

Dev Anand & Rajesh Khanna were the superstars those days and they set fashion trends, hairstyles, dressing & speaking. Rajesh Khanna's open jeep song with Sharmila Tagore on a train in Darjeeling, with Rajesh Khanna wearing a V cut Jacket styled without buttons & pocket in "Mere Sapno Ki Rani" was a fashion many adopted. How come our Players would not fall for it? Father got made the same Jacket for himself which was born by the youngest son who made a fusion with Dev Anand's hairstyle & Rajesh Khanna's Jacket. So open Jeep & this Jacket, the song in heart relived.

There was this 'Willy Jeep' which could be converted to an open jeep and also had a trolley for carrying luggage. Commuting was thru rickshaws and long distance within the city mostly thru horse-driven Tonga. Outstation or family outing Jeep was used. The cycle was mostly a personal carrier for errands, rides to school, college, office & workplace. Cycling & cycle racing were a free time, more fun than exercise. Kids were sportier in the absence of other time waste activities.

Air Conditioners/ air coolers were not there but Fans yes, Ceiling and table. Mostly preferred to sleep in the open due to heat & to safeguard against mosquitos/ flies there were mosquito nets used alongside a table fan. Electricity was quite erratic so mostly hand fans were used.

The housewife's hobby of farming really provided the household with fresh veggies straight from the surrounding field and even wheat crop cultivation. The field was prepared for sowing using a tractor equipped with a tilling trolley and sharp disc blades for tilling. For farming and gardening, help was retained. Along with farming, Cow Keeping was also there with two cows. Kutty machine- manual was there for making feed for cows. It was an event when cows delivered baby calf. Nothing less than bringing up your own child. Mother Cow's love and care for calf was to be seen to be believed.

A self-sustaining individual economy of sorts. Cow milk for dairy products, cow dung to make upla- dung cakes to fuel chulha (manual stove) since cooking gas was not available. There were kerosene stoves but kerosene was rationed. Farming used to yield fodder for cows with other nutrients were added separately. All vegetable like Potato, Carrot, Reddish, Tomato, Chili, coriander, cauliflower, lady finger, brinjal etc. were grown in filed itself. Wheat used to be sufficient till next crop.

The house lady defined 'ENOUGH' and accordingly built eco system to reach it. Greed has no limits and place if one wish to be happy & peaceful in life.

After paying for things like farming and other costs, the wage generated was therefore somewhat conserved. All of these benefits came with the job. Back then, the middle class could afford the lifestyle; today, only the extremely wealthy can. Along with benefits, the position included a free weekly elephant ride. Wagons carrying merchandise were pushed inside the plant by elephants. Every Sunday, these elephants received a special diet. It was administered at the bungalow in front of the housekeeper in order to prevent thefts of this diet. Elephants would be brought to a bungalow where a mahout or mahavat would cook food in their presence and then present it to the elephants. Everyone presents, even the house lady, offered the diet. An enjoyable treat was the elephant ride at the conclusion. Love & care has no language but it is acknowledged by all entities be it humans, animals or plants. You take care of them and they blossom.

One day a Cow Elephant came to the bungalow alone in search of food as she may be hungry. Noticing, the house lady gathered Kutty- the cow feed and spread it on the raised flat platform – Chabootra for Cow Elephant. She tried to make a pile of it to make it easy for Cow elephants to eat. But Cow Elephant could not wait and gently pushed the lady with trunk to one side. But a gentle push turned out to be a kind of blow making the lady fell on the ground. Cow Elephant little bit backtracked and did not eat till the lady got up and again made a pile of Kutty - fodder. Cow Elephant ate, by the time mahout came & she went back.

Milking the cows was quite interesting. Most of the time house lady used to do it. Normally while milking rear legs are tied to avoid movement. But when the house lady used to milk, cows used to stand straight despite having flies disturbing them. The house lady had given clear instructions to first let cows feed their calf to the extent the calf is satisfied and then the remaining milk was to be milked. The remaining milk was ENOUGH for family needs. The mother cows obviously noticed it and allowed milking happily knowing their calf's hunger has been satiated. Milking was done twice a day. There was this fierce cow called Shyama, everyone feared going near her. Her feed was prepared & served keeping her at a distance. But she too was so friendly with the house lady that sometimes out of love gesture she would place her front legs on the house lady's shoulders while sitting, she prepared feed.

It was a blessed upbringing for the Players in similar or better socio-economic life-styled aspirational neighborhoods. They faced both a blessed upbringing and an average life with hand to mouth situation. This probably instilled an understanding of the value of being blessed and made them humble and caring.

They did not know their life would unfold so differently being impacted by time, period & environment, and their choices thereafter in quest for growth, security & a happy life.

The Astrologer, Mining Engineer & a Journalist

What you love to do - hobby, what you wish to become - dream & what you become - duty is a matter of how life unfolds. It is rare that all three – Hobby, Dream & Duty become ONE and get unified. Yes, these may confluence and overlap sometimes or most of the times but may not be always. Either Fall in love & marry or Marry & fall in love with spouse. If 1st is not happening, 2nd is always best and most rewarding.

A decision has to be made, is it 'ENOUGH' to follow Hobby, a Dream or Duty in order to not only survive but thrive peacefully?

We feel such outcomes are forced by circumstances but the fact is that the outcomes are the result of our decisions made in those circumstances. No decision made is wrong or right. Everyone makes the best decision basis the best understanding, knowledge and circumstance while deciding. It is always wrong to tag a past decision as wrong or correct. Circumstances & situations throw an opportunity & a challenge to decide, to make a choice. That's where defining 'ENOUGH' and managing expectations play a crucial role to make the best possible decision.

The four boys of money lander were all different even though with the same upbringing. The eldest enjoyed all privileges of being rich. His friend circle included legendary actor Pran, the most famous villain ever, Pran Sahib as popularly known in Bollywood. His father was serving the British government and had a transferable job. In matriculation, both Pran & the eldest son got into a friendship which lasted till the next posting of Pran's father & becomes a tale. The youngest two were treated as kids all through their adolescence & struggled to gain a foothold in the real world. Their wives groomed their prodigies knowing the shortcomings of their fathers & are doing so well in their lives, fulfilling family responsibilities and building their own lives. To well educate children, and make them sensitive & responsible was 'ENOUGH' for the wives at that time.

Change is possible by knowing what is to be corrected & how, what is to be achieved i.e. 'ENOUGH' & how to go about it. The journey is always small steps forward to success.

The second boy Rupert's intuition and the company he kept or selected undoubtedly had an influence on his life. While he also had all the benefits, his preference was for academics.

To the point of blind trust, astrology and astrologers were an essential element of family life and consulted for every conceivable event or broad prognostications. Rupert of-course observed and got inclined to learn astrology. At 13 years of age Rupert started to learn astrology and in years to come became proficient with the help of a family astrologer. By reading a lot of books on astrology, palmistry & numerology he further honed his skills.

He always kept it to a hobby and decided not to make a living out of it. It was his thinking to give back to society by helping them with future indications and possible solutions for making planetary movements favorable or less impacting by way of prayers and putting on stones or crystal. He always treated astrology as science based on mathematical calculations of the planetary movement & zodiac signs. Any astrologer can do the math but important was the interpretations thus predicting & relating it to a native's position, time, period & environment. This art of interpretation and prediction comes by reading, understanding and practice exactly like a medical practitioner the more experienced & learned the better doctor.

Rupert used to strongly warn people not to place their complete trust on astrological forecasts and to keep up their efforts. He believed that while corrective measures do not totally eliminate suffering, they do offer one more endurance. He encouraged people to utilize astrology as a "road map" to avoid making decisions that would not be fruitful and to make efforts in the appropriate direction at the appropriate time. Today that's what we do with the help of Google Maps, we sort of predict the fastest and safest way to go anywhere. Rupert was an unconventional Karma yogi who valued action during a time when the majority of people had other ideas. He learnt Sanskrit, Marathi & Urdu to gain knowledge thru related literature in these languages. He turned out to be an avid reader. He had a large collection of books in astrology, palmistry & numerology which got donated to a library after he was gone. His books shall all be kept in a particular order on bookshelves, which was well memorized & he would pick up the desired book straight away without having to search for it.

Since it was a hobby & he did not charge, anyone who came to him through a reference was obliged with straight feedback and confidence building. His 'ENOUGH' was to help people & did not make it a profession. He wanted people to know & use astrology as a science which could indicate rough patches and good patches of life & how to face these. Rupert made a mark & was respected by people, friends & anyone who came in contact with him for his thoughts, vision & conduct.

1930 to 1940 was the most active decade of industrial growth*, where KGF- Kollar Gold Field, Hospet, Bellary etc. (in post-Independence Karnataka State) were in the limelight for mining, textile & other industry growth. (*Ref https://dokumen.tips/documents/chapter-a-149-kolar-gold-field-mining-mysore-iron-and-steel-factory-sandal.html)

One can always dream big & probably the money lender thought for taking up a mine. Who shall manage & fulfil this dream? Rupert was asked to do mining engineering. He joined BHU the Benaras Hindu University for a Mining Engineering degree.

The fact that this industry of money lending does not have a future in a rapidly changing world was obvious to the money lender. Although independence was evident, many people undoubtedly weren't sure how it would affect the situation. There was a need for alternative business, a company that could provide for a large family of more than 20–25 individuals for the rest of their lives. The then local State authorities took no ominous or prognosticative steps regarding modernization and industrialization, which may result in improved &

diversified economic possibilities. Probably, mining came to be a business option at that time, a dreamy thought as it seems now. But for sure complete mathematics must have been done by a money lender. The joint family's future hinged on Rupert's Mining Engineering.

Another genesis for Rupert's mining engineering decision could have also been there. It was clear to the money lender that this money lending business does not hold future in fast changing time, period and environment. He knew his eldest son, who completed schooling and was fluent in English would sail through. Younger two would require support which he would support. About Rupert, he was good at studies could have a promising future if he becomes an engineer given the changing economic scene and ensuing industrialization. Thus, result was mining engineering from Benaras Hindu University – a prestigious institution. "Parents want the best for children" hasn't changed for ages.

Whatever the genesis behind the engineering decision, the 'ENOUGH' defined was to become an engineer, it was achievable also given the intellect level and money to afford it. 'Enough' was to make Rupert stand on his feet and live a well respectable life.

The independence movement became fervent & everyone even though having varied ideologies and beliefs came together with one mission Full Freedom, Complete Independence - 'Quit India'. The Hindu Nationalist movement also gathered momentum and started spreading its ideology to unite, strengthen, safeguard & propagate Hindu culture and preserve the glorious past by spreading knowledge & creating awareness through weekly discussions in groups.

Their mass contact program included meeting students at colleges and aligning them to the purpose of uniting the Hindu population & modernize their deep-rooted orthodox thinking e.g. to bring untouchables to the mainstream. Shaping up young minds to preserve Hindu culture & traditions was a way to broaden the movement. While they looked at the increase of member base, in particular, they focused on brilliant youngsters from affluent families for a far better impact on Hindu society. Once a member, affiliation was for lifetime but the member was free to pursue other movements or congregation etc. Many members chose to dedicate their full lives to this cause by remaining single.

These Hindu Nationalist movements covertly strengthened the freedom struggle by way of the united awakening of the majority community. It also seeded harmony by creating a balance of power. Harmony was frequently disturbed as an outcome of the 'divide & rule' policy of British rulers.

Rupert got indoctrinated with the idea & believed that Bharat can flourish the Hindu way which is democratic having tolerance, and strength to lead being the oldest & most progressed/ advanced religion worldwide. Like each other countrymen he too wanted freedom...poorna swaraj. He completed his engineering and dedicated himself to this cause. He was in the company of brilliant and promising young minds who later reached the echelon of power in their own domain & participated in mainstream nation-building. Most of them did not marry for the cause. Rupert while evaluating his options decided to get married yet continue for this mission to strengthen and awaken Hindus. He completely dedicated his first 14 years of married life to this cause.

The objectives of the Hindu Nationalist movements were not restricted to Independence but to build a strong Nation with values and learnings of Hinduism, the oldest religion & way of life on earth. To do that movement's mentors allocated fields to their lifetime members to achieve create a like-minded environment and keep the objective alive to be fulfilled & create a balance in Nation's life. Therefore, members were assigned social services, education, politics, journalism, civil services, bureaucracy & other pillars of democracy. Rupert even though engineer by qualification was assigned Journalism.

During this time, every person in India shown patriotism and made contributions to it to the best of their ability. Not an exception was Rupert. His calling was to become a journalist, which he became, and he served the cause of the Hindu Nationalist movement with unwavering dedication and honesty throughout his life.

His hobby was to practice astrology, and he became a good one. His dream was to become an engineer, and he became one. His duty was to become a Journalist and he became one.

The Love, Marriage & the Wait

Rupert, like many other young, ambitious, wealthy lads, intended to dedicate his entire life to serving the Hindutva mission while remaining single and unmarried. His mentor questioned if he could and should leave his mission and advised him to think things over before making any decision. On the hostel wall, two lines were drawn: one for "Yes" (for marriage) and the other for "No," denoting the choice. Each line battled the other in a protracted conflict that was depicted on the wall. So many lines were sacrificed before 'Yes' was declared the winner. Sharon lived in same mohalla as Rupert. Their houses were separated by two big houses in between. This was a mohalla of the rich and affluent. By now Rupert's virtues became known and appreciated. It was a big feat to become an engineer.

Sharon was the third child of five surviving siblings. Her father popularly called Choudhary Sahib, was senior treasurer with the Nawab. Theirs was a religious family & every evening there would be a congregation of elders singing bhajan and praying Lord. She was quite a pampered child. Her mother had to keep an empty glass near her bed to prove in the morning that she was given milk at night otherwise she would create a ruckus. Sharon called her parents Chacha and Chachi instead of Babu ji (father) & Amma (mother). This was because she grew up listening her elder cousins calling her parents as Chacha ji & Chachi ji. After 3rd standard, she refused to go to school and Chacha & Chachi buckled, she being pampered child. Every evening she would participate in choir in her house and got religiously inclined. Sharon grew into a beautiful pious woman with a wheatish complexion. She got so involved intoning hymns - bhajans, actually started to write these and a breviary (gutka) of hymns was printed. Her virtues became known and appreciated.

Sharon & Rupert had glanced at each other many a times, every time they looked at each other, they wanted more of such glances. Sharon would find herself on the balcony waiting for that enamored look. While they never spoke to each other or tried a rendezvous despite being in the same mohalla with many opportunities if they wanted to. The look alone was a great healer/pacifier for both.

The first opportunity both got they spilled the beans to their families about fascination for each other. Her parents though told her about Rupert's commitment to Hindutva mission, cautioned that her family life may have hiccups. Sharon was more vocal to her Chacha & Chachi that if it is not Rupert then no one! The families were joyous and the marriage occurred. She was convinced that Rupert being a committed, honest person with high values shall take good care of family.

She had first taste of life unfolding when Rupert preferred to go for his daily scheduled morning congregation instead of taking his bride home to participate in Bidai ceremony. He asked Bidai to be done with his 'laathi' instead. Elders intervened and the Bidai ceremony was performed with Rupert. The laathi became part of Rupert clan homes being not only a weapon of protection but also a symbol of their parents' love.

She got acquainted with her lover's passion & commitment to his mission, and what ensued was the wait of almost 14 years to be together. Rupert was assigned to Gorakhpur for propagating the Hindu Nationalist movement's objective. He would come back home once a year and sometimes even once in two years. Every time they met, their love manifested in offspring. They remain committed to & love each other. Letters were the only method of communicate.

Money lender's all four daughters in laws were given a room & common area of their own on the first floor of the house. The three lived with their husbands. Sharon became completely merged with the joint family doing household chores and bringing up the kids. The kitchen for this joint family was common and each daughter-in-law contributed to the well-being of the family. The love of in-laws & routine helped in this time of waiting for reunion & being together.

Rupert followed strict routine and actions as prescribed for the vision and mission of Hindutva. There in Gorakhpur he met many renowned personalities.

The name "Gorakhpur" comes from the Sanskrit Gorakshapuram, which means abode of Gorakhnath, a renowned ascetic who was a prominent saint of the Nath Sampradaya.

The geographical form of Gorakhpur City is that of a bowl since it is situated on the basin of the rivers Rapti and Rohini. Cool Rapti River protects the city's west side, while magnificent Sal Forest, which is located on the east, provides a sublime sense of calm and a cool wind at all times. The emerald Ramgarh Tal in the south is a shower of perfection, while the north serves as the foundation for the growth of the city. Gorakhpur has its own cultural and historical importance. It is the birthplace of Firaq

Gorakhpuri, the workplace of writer Sh. Munshi Premchand and mystic poet Kabirdas. Associated with Gautam Buddha and Lord Mahavir, Martyr Pt. Ram Prasad Bismil, Bandhu Singh and many more. Only a naïve would currently not relate to Gorakhpur with Yogi Aditya Nath ji.

Gorakhpur was a part of the famous kingdom of Koshal, one of sixteen mahajanpadas in the 6th Century B.C. The earliest known monarch ruling over this region with his capital at Ayodhya was IKSVAKU, who founded the solar dynasty of Kshatriya. It produced a number of illustrations kings till the accession of Ram, who was the greatest ruler of this dynasty. Since then, it remained an integral part of the erstwhile empires of Maurya, Shunga, Kushana, Gupta and Harsha dynasties. (Gorakhpur.nic.in).

During Gorakhpur's stay, Rupert got an opportunity to meet Shri Hanuman Prasad ji Poddar. He was an independence activist, littérateur, magazine editor and philanthropist. He was the founding editor of the spiritual magazine in Hindi- Kalyan, which was published by Gita Press setup by Ghanshyam Jalan and Jay Dayal ji Goeyendka.

Kalyan was a way to spread the spiritual glory and heroic deeds of heroes of the Ramayana and the Mahabharata amongst each Indian so that they feel spiritually free and proud of their achievements in the past & to act as a source of inspiration to fight for the independence of India.

He dedicated his life to making available great epics like the Ramayana, the Mahabharata, the Puranas and the Upanishads translated into Hindi to the common people at affordable prices.

'Kalyan' has published special issues on all Puranas, Upanishads and on many more subjects related to Hindu culture and religion.

He wrote many books on spiritual and value-oriented subjects in Hindi and English. In his translation of some Upanishads and Puranas, he has taken care of the communicability of the language to the common people without causing any compromise with their poetic and philosophical heights and depths. Interestingly it is said by his near ones that while having any doubt with regards to any God or Goddess, the Gods and goddesses would appear before him and clear the doubts. It was also said that while he recited Ramayana, Anjani putra Shri Hanuman ji would come to listen to it, it was so melodious and filled with bhakti.

Lovingly called Bhaijee, he was a multifaceted personality. As an editor of the religious magazine 'Kalyan', he is known for his untiring efforts to propagate and disseminate Hinduism across the world.

His work in fostering pride among the people regarding India's history and philosophic tradition earned him praise from Mahatma Gandhi.

This meeting turned out to be an unexpected help in form of Bhai ji in guiding & mentoring Rupert with another dimension to spread awareness thru journalism. Taking the tips, Rupert got associated as an Editor of a bimonthly magazine in home town the Nawab State capital. This was on an honorary basis.

Rupert's ENOUGH was to work for propagating Hindu values and culture which he dedicated himself to. But then he had taken up a family and had also to look after them. It was time that he had to redefine his expectation of himself, others & family in particular. Time flies and the past seems so simple & possible in present.

It was the start of the 60s that Rupert moved to a bigger city becoming a correspondent with a leading English daily newspaper then. To be one of the founding members of the city edition. This time entire family accompanied him. This was a period when China waged war with India. India was badly beaten & defeated. India post-independence in 1947 was still gathering herself & defining the way forward, when this war took place.

His salary was Rs.13 per month at that time which would mean roughly about Rs.1125/ today with an approx. the average annual inflation rate of 7.4% considered. Mathematically though it may be a correct correlation but if you ask senior citizens in their 70s (or refer online search) they would tell that things were quite cheap then e.g. golgappa or paanipuri then was 'one golgappa' for 'one paisa' and today it is minimum five hundred paise (Rs.5/-) for one, sugar was approx. 40 paisa / Seer i.e. 1.25 Kg, potato approx. 25 paisa/kg, atta approx. 10 paisa/kg, milk approx. 12 paisa/ltr, dal was 20 paisa/kg & rice was 12 paisa/kg so on & so forth. The cost of living was quite less then. Still, Rs.13/- per month salary was a tight rope walk - hand to mouth situation. They knew that they are doing their best and had ENOUGH to sail through, no point complaining.

Except for the medical challenge of two children, they all were happily living & learning new things. One day Rupert brought Bread & butter for breakfast. Sharon did not know what to do with it so as usual she baked it in on tava and like roti with butter. ☺. Until a friend from BHU days told them how bread butter is prepared & doesn't need to be baked if the toaster is not available. These can be taken directly from the pack.

People were very kind, and they always received unanticipated assistance when they needed it, whether it came in the shape of a nurse going above and beyond in her care of her sick kid or a doctor regularly visiting homes without charging a home visit charge or a reduced clinic visit price.

Sharon was learning about life and a tightrope balance between needs and available finance, managing growing children & keeping her love alive and thriving.

'The Wait' does not seem to leave her life as Rupert had a busy working schedule and being a journalist had to be quite social to stay relevant. She used to wait for him to return and the next day again leaves early morning for the congregation and office work.

The Wait had become an integral part of her routine. There was hardly any 'Me Time' with her but she never grudged and happily carried on family life. She however kept herself updated and relevant with times. She found her ENOUGH in raising kids imbibing values, culture & ethics in their upbringing. Whatever time they spent together became ENOUGH for her knowing Rupert's passion for whatever he decided to do. She did not complain.

The Knowledge & Efforts Never Go Waste

The money lender called back Rupert and exhorted him to take up a profession basis his degree. He was clear in his message that now freedom has come & it is enough of Hindutva work. It can still continue but more focus is required on career specially having a big family of seven surviving children & their future needs to be secured. He was getting old and wanted his children to settle down properly. He believed that if children are wise they don't need wealth & if they are fool wealth shall not last long. Wealth requires a 'WILL' to be made but Sanskar – culture makes a 'GOODWILL'.

Rupert never shied from taking up work in the quest to look after the family. Though he never was inclined to earn too much & only wanted to be able to sustain himself without debt. Be it work of supervising mud laying to create a base for airstrip or working in Karnataka – Hospet mines or returning back to his home town to look after ageing parents, finding a job in home town multitasking – administration, union management, legal obligations etc. Facing office politics, changing jobs and finally landing in the capital to manage a multilingual news agency as Chief News Editor.

He took his work to heart which lead to health complications like high blood pressure leading to heart issues. His last ten or so years of life were spent at home largely, sometimes even bedridden but with a fully active mind. This was the time when his daughter Angie took great care of him like any son would have, even much better than that. 'Daughters are no less than a Son' got validation once again. He never came in way of the career of any of his children and allowed them to move out to different cities despite being in precarious health conditions.

He never attempted to create wealth. The best wealth was his friend circle, the friends who respected him & liked him. What were those values for which his friends never gave up supporting him & his family till his last breath and till settling down the youngest son? He had access to 24X7 medical access without actually bothering about payment at checkout time. While all bills were settled though late. His friend circle also included a tailor at a posh market. He did not ask for money for tailoring and it was payable when able. Actually, people around were sure that their money is safe but shall come late. This 'payable when able' facility was actually due to friends who valued relationships. His life was that of a Giver & Taker but he never thought as Equalizer. The remaining debts and obligations were repaid with gratitude by Sharon. Friends and well-wishers did not wish to take back what was given out of mutual respect & not to be returned but she requested. She did not wish Rupert to be remembered finally as a Taker alone. Credibility must be maintained even if one is no more. This act of hers further enhanced the prestige of Rupert & his family.

Influential people were in his circle of friends. But he never requested a favor from any of them. Always up front, highly ethical, objectively and unflinching in his opinions, kind-hearted, supportive to the very end, and never afraid to ask for favors for others; selfless worker; always a giver; humble and down to earth; no egos; highly optimistic; action-oriented; strong will power; and resilient. During his health-wise difficult times, over the last ten years, he did not expect the way support poured in for him. He learnt astrology at 13 years of age, mastered it over time & this hobby got him the required money as a retention amount on monthly basis at a time when he needed the most. His journalism skills supported him in publishing articles & writing radio talk shows which fetched a remuneration. The people he supported came back to support him. There was this friend of his who gave a one-hour-a-day job to his son (so that he can continue his studies) in his office for a pay to support. He did not have savings/ wealth but none of his requirements got stuck due to lack of money. Almighty has his own designs to support and lead a respectable life. The best thing that happened to him was Sharon. She did manage within available scope the family expenses.

Settling down children & marrying them is considered to be the onus and responsibility of parents in our society. It was the last 10 years of Rupert's life that he & Sharon had to see through this responsibility. Each of their children were struggling, hustling to the best scope of their ability & inching towards earning progress. Rupert's movements were restricted so someone had to take up his role & handle responsibilities instead.

Bree was the brightest Son of all four sons securing distinction throughout. He was quite influenced by Rupert's way of life & somewhere developed a latent wish to be loved & respected like Rupert in family & social circles. He followed Rupert's footsteps joined the Hindutva Nationalist Movement & became active. Got himself arrested during the emergency period, and released with a warning then. The officer had empathy for the young boy's career & did not wish to blot it.

Bree wanted to further study which Rupert could not afford. So, he decided to do it on his own & started giving private tuition to fund higher studies. He followed a hectic schedule in order to have ENOUGH for the purpose. In this period, he got a fantastic friend circle of hustlers and achievers.

Bree took initiative & assumed responsibility in all family matters & five of seven siblings got married in these last 10 years of Rupert's life much to his relief. Bree actually came to be a Grown-up even to elders- the chaperone of the family taking care and supporting. The fact is God provides every family with a 'Bree' who chaperones in hours of need.

Rupert died a satisfied man in peace because he had defined his 'ENOUGH' at every stage of his life. That 'ENOUGH' was right or wrong, no one should judge. Life is such a darling that even in its worst form one wants to live, so to say that Rupert did not have much left to do would be wrong. He would have but his ENOUGH gave him satisfaction of what he did and with so many people unexpectedly helping him was itself satisfying that God watched him. He did his karma.

Did he die happy? Ask his family & friends, they would say YES. Because they never found him complaining, morose, unhappy & sad. He did his efforts and enjoyed whatever the outcomes were. He has been a hustler all thru his life & a believer in Geeta -

The verse from Shrimad Bhagwat Geeta –

कर्मण्येवाधिकारस्ते मा फलेषु कदाचन।

मा कर्मफलहेतुर्भूर्मा ते सङ्गोऽस्त्वकर्मणि॥ २-४७

In roman script -

Karmanye vadhikaraste Ma Phaleshu Kadachana,

Ma Karmaphalaheturbhurma Te Sangostvakarmani

The translation –

You have the right to work only but never to its fruits. Let not the fruits of action be your motive, nor let your attachment be to inaction.

His off springs / prodigies had to chalk out their own course of life. They did not inherit wealth but definitely inherited culture, knack of judging right or wrong, action orientation & resilience, strong will power, positivity, emotional strength & purpose orientation.

The Wife & the Mother

Sharon's life journey was even more challenging throughout. It was her belief in God which gave strength to her. She had a strong will power and always believed in efforts & actions rather than worrying & pointing her fate.

Out of seven children a son suffered polio & a daughter suffered nerve issue, she could not bend her leg and run, barely could walk.

She always believed & followed below verse which is a conversation between Shiva & Parvati as mentioned in Ramcharitramanas -

होइहि सोइ जो राम रचि राखा। को करि तर्क बढ़ावै साखा॥

In roman English-

Hoi hai soi jo Ram rachi rakha, ko kari tarak baravahin sakha".

The meaning –

Whatever Shri Ram has willed must come to pass; why should one add to complication by indulging in further speculation?

She believed to face & sail through what shall come rather than blaming fate. If one is destined to suffer no one can help to avoid that suffering & if one is destined to flourish no one can harm or create roadblocks.

One must keep walking, be resilient, keep putting effort, persist & persist. Manage expectations according to time, period and environment. This belief kept her at ease all the time & she enjoyed the results of her efforts & played her part in life's journey happily. Her contentment was with the best efforts she made rather than the outcome.

The experiences of life can make you strong and equally can weaken you. At every stage of their life she faced tough challenges which she faced with a firm belief in efforts. Every time some unforeseen & unexpected help was at hand to support her sail through these challenges. To the extent that she believed nothing would go wrong and if suffering have come, it is destiny. Every night lasts till morning & it is a continuous cycle of nature.

Rupert was not able to spend more time with family in his quest for life. Sharon always yearned for more time together. How this could be achieved. She learnt to play card games like Bridge, Paplu Rummy etc, so that she can accompany him to clubs & socialize. She also learnt English speaking to be able to converse in social gatherings. She got so engrossed in learning English that one day during pooja she muttered Ram ji AND Sita ji ko namaskar instead of regular prayer Ram ji AUR Sita ji ko namaskar! ☺. She did efforts & whatever time she could spend together became ENOUGH for her. She never complained about the Wait she endured all through till the last 10 years of Rupert. During these 10 years, they were together and rediscovered their love. She took extreme care.

Today, to increase TRPs, likes almost everyone is using 'Sympathy' as a tool. Stories of penury, from rags-to-rich about socially successful people in various fields do rounds on social media attracting millions of likes. Just reiterating that there is 'n' no of success stories, if we look around and acknowledge these. These players may not have social acclaims & fame but are happy with their achievements in tough times.

Friends and family of Sharon always found her cheerful, forward looking, enthusiastic & action oriented. Any ordinary person would have buckled under pressure, it's her will power and love for life that kept her moving all the time. She never showed any signs of seeking Sympathy or using her plight to ask/expect favors.

One can easily comprehend how a daunting task it would have been to raise seven children with two having medical challenges. There were times of plenty with farming, cow keeping and a bungalow with all facilities. There were times of penury when it was hand to mouth situation. God lines up everything & sends unexpected helps. There was a milkman shop adjacent & a grocery one in opposite house. When there was nothing to give children, she would get milk & breads, buns as a onetime meal. Other meals included namak mirch ka parantha with homemade pickle and curd some times. Whatever parantha or roti would remain, she would prepare dahi ki roti.

Month's beginning was ok as she would repay last month bill and buy fresh on credit. She rotated the credit, giving 1st priority to repayment than others expenses. Payment at promised time created credit worthiness & she kept getting same. There was an advantage with clothing requirements of family. Having seven of them same clothes from eldest sibling to youngest got used with little adjustment. She would use her waste sarees to make shirts for children which actually became a fashion in mohalla. There were many food hacks she would apply like making small namak jeera muthry served with tea as a meal. Idea was to fill the belly. Whenever, rice was made, it's maad – rice bran or rice water was served to drink. Generally, this is thrown. Its health benefits were latent. One day her son-in-law (damaad ji) dropped in. She just prepared rice water, rice, namak ka prantha and normal grass chutney. He was well to do but knew the situation. He had a great taste & was fond of good food. He enjoyed & relished the meal and asked her what all this was. She never hid the reality & openly shared the ingredients. He laughed & appreciated the taste. He never felt tired of narrating this story ever with lot of respect for her.

She has always been a hustler believed in efforts & try it out mindset. To settle eldest son who did not do well in studies, she started a shop in partnership. It did not work out. She then bought tractor to be rented out for farming, did not work out. Lastly, she realized ENOUGH for her son and let him work in a godam – warehouse as store keeper. He had to cycle more than 15 km one way every day for work & returned tired, exhausted. His hustle got started. Each of her child became a hustler but common virtues were patience, effort, resilience, willpower & optimism.

Managing a life of nine persons with only one person's earnings was an absolute challenge. However, her common sense, good intents, practical approach and finance rotation out of inherited gold, helped her sail thru all critical times. She managed expectations, defined what ENOUGH for the time was and acted. Like no one knows what's in store in future? She had focused her energies on the present.

Gold has always been a savior in challenging times & it is even today. Recent news tells that Indian Women hold 11% of the world's gold with them. A mix of both sources – inheritance and wealth creation. When money lender passed away without a 'Will'. All siblings sat together & divided everything the jewelry, properties, farms, cattle & other household valuable. Most siblings were not satisfied with the division but there was no option but to accept.

Rupert got 14 houses & some jewelry. Whenever any of his sibling approached Rupert for financial help he handed over documents of a house asking them to sell it and make money. There was no other way to extend help. Only one house got left since it could not be sold being occupied by a government agency.

Sharon did not allow inherited gold to be given since she knew it was the only security she had for the future. Unlike today when there are so many ways to have financial security thru savings in Mutual Funds, Equity etc. it was mostly gold and land that provided social security for difficult times in life.

The inherited jewelry had one necklace with 8 bigger and 16 smaller pendants. She made eight necklaces set out of it for her seven children and herself. Remaining pieces of jewelry remained intact and was used to fund all emergencies and bigger expenses like marriages. The big support came from her elder cousin and younger sibling, both were rich.

She would pledge gold with them and borrow money on interest. Every time, interest was paid on schedule. She would borrow from the other again and refund the principal on time if she did not have the funds to pay back the principal on the agreed-upon date. Gold that had been pledged to them both stayed with her and was never handed to them.

She would monitor gold prices and sell gold when its price paid for the interest and principal as well as provided some additional cash. She was guided by this rotation through a trying time. Of course, over time, her gold fortune continued to diminish, but it was nevertheless used to support her and meet other obligations.

It is with the help of Rupert's friends after his demise that the only house remained of property inheritance got vacated by the government body and got sold for a good price. This money gave her the strength and support needed during her last years. Though, by this time all her children had become self-reliant & took good care of hers. She was to endure more pains in her last days in the form of the demise of her second son, his wife leaving behind two kids and eldest son-in-law. She got love and respect and some solace after a tortuous, hassled & hustled life. It was her wish that her last journey should not have inadequacy & all rituals must be performed properly.

As luck would have it, the day she died at her youngest son's home, he did not have any money in hand or in the bank. The doctor who came to see her and declared her demise did not charge any fee. He was a family doctor and knew everyone. At the time of her last breath, her eldest daughter happens to be with her.

Unexpected help came through with a call from Citibank call center asking if a personal loan of Rs.25000/- is required as it was eligible on the credit card. The youngest son did not blink & accepted a request for the draft to be sent by the same day evening or the next day morning narrating the situation. It came through and the bank also en-cashed it.

Now there was ENOUGH in hand to complete all ceremonies and rituals for the last journey of his beloved mother without inadequacy/lackluster. On the last day of 'Garun Purana' completion while Aarti was being performed her youngest son heard her voice singing the Aarti "Om Jai Jagdeesh Hare....", he looked around to see if she was there but could not see her. Probably it was a sign that she parted fully satisfied.

A Gold That Didn't Glitter

India was proclaimed a polio-free nation in February 2014. The action began in 1995. Polio used to be a fatal illness. The polio vaccine wasn't created until approximately 1955, and the oral drop for polio wasn't created until 1961. Approximately 2 lac cases of polio were reported per year in India throughout the 1970s and 1980s. Polio has no known treatment; the only way to avoid it is by getting vaccinated repeatedly. Typically, children under the age of five are affected. Typically, it causes permanent paralysis in the legs and kills 5–10% of afflicted infants.

Benson the 2nd son of seven siblings got affected by this disease. Polio affected his left leg which stopped developing, practically became lifeless & dangling leg from the hip. He would not feel anything in this leg. An underarm crutch was made by a carpenter with a length from an inch lower to armpit to feet. A curved handle/top to act as support was placed under the armpit and a cylindrical handle was rabbeted at around the hip to be held by the left hand to support body weight lean on the left side. To be more stable body weight was to be rested on the arm using the handgrip & not on top of the crutch under the arm. Otherwise, it could damage the shoulder. The base of the crutch was so designed to avoid skidding. It was to be learnt how much pressure to exhort and how to put a crutch on the floor to avoid skidding. While walking instead of the left foot it was the crutch that would come forward taking on full body weight while leaning left allowing the right leg to move forward taking up full body weight then allowing the left crutch to move forward. Left shoulder and hand became strong to be able to take on the pressure of walking. The whole motion had to be synced for a pace to be kept. The dangling leg was to be placed or jammed at the intersection of two sides joint to one rod, just below the hand grip. This was necessary so that while walking the dangling leg does not interfere or get entangled to obstruct movement. Now of course one can buy aluminum crutches but at that time it was made of wood by local carpenters duly smoothened for comfort not polished though. The color was real wood. Carpentry at its best.

A boy who had just learnt to walk much to the happiness of parents and elder siblings got affected by Polio, crutch became part of body for rest of his life. There was no alternate but to learn to live with it. So, he did not treat this as deficiency & it became a new normal to him. It was like a pair of shoe or a dress with increasing size till the body attained full height. So, the crutch kept growing from small to large in line with body size.

A brave heart from childhood itself. He got serious pus formation in his body and it had to be syringed out without anesthesia. Only those who endure can experience pain. No written or verbal expression can even reach near to actual pain. Mother would ask him if he wish to go to war with China then he would have to take this treatment, and Benson would agree to endure that unbearable pain.

He was quite a handsome boy, one would get attracted to him at first sight itself with such an innocent face. He was no less in any way than a normal person. His dressing sense was attractive despite a dangling leg. He would wear normal trousers & fold the left side to the shortened length of the leg. Put on shoes on both feet. He wore normal shirts which were torn off faster from the left armpit due to constant rubbing with the crutch top.

He did everything to increase his confidence quotient. He practices cycling with one leg & was the fastest among his friends & brothers. He played cricket and was a good hitter of the ball. He did bowl as well with a small run-up.

He did play 'chidi chakka' - badminton and remain unbeatable amongst his friends and brothers. He played table tennis at inter-college level to become a State runner-up. He shined more because of his efforts at perfection with a disability rather than the sympathy of others which he never wanted.

A daredevil by nature right from bearing the pain of pus extraction by a big syringe, to driving Willy the jeep with an elder on the left side to manage clutch to ghost hunting midnight. He was the strongman of the house ready to take on any challenge or fight to safeguard family. He adopted the look of a strongman with the handlebar & at times the Hungarian moustaches, of course did go to Akhara/dojo for body training & building.

He also got a dagger/knife made especially so that it can be concealed tied with a belt on the right leg on top of socks just above the ankle & covered with trousers' leg opening at cuffs. A dagger or knife has a very sharp point and usually two sharp edges. Typically, designed or capable of being used as a thrusting or stabbing weapon, daggers have been used throughout human history for close combat confrontations and often fulfilled a secondary defense weapon's role.

Daggers have a short blade with a sharply tapered point, a central spine or fuller, and usually, two cutting edges sharpened the full length of the blade. Though most daggers featured a full cross guard, this one had a small apt for hand grip.

This dagger had no sharp edges, both side edges were quite blunt and could not even cut a paper. It was only to show and shoo away rivals as it actually looked deadly. He did make friends with people who behaved like bully boys, did smoke, drink & eat non-veg as any young fellow would occasionally do in the company of like-minded people.

These habits were not acceptable as a family norm. His father asked him to stop these habits & promise not to do it ever. Benson did not budge after a couple of warnings. To reprimand, father out of anger started caning at his back. This cane was made of Rattan palm called natural dragon rattan cane, and flexible & hard-hitting. The rattan stalks are harvested and the thorns along with joints are detached and the bark is alienated from the core. The bark of the rattan is used in producing thin strips of cane. These are cylindrical with even diameters, flexible and long. Benson kept bearing the brunt of caning but did not utter that what he was doing shall not be repeated. His back had so many bruises with blood about to ooze out. Normally, children don't see their father cry but that day everyone saw it, a mentally tough father broke down but not the son.

He threw the cane and applied medicine at Benson's back. For so many days Benson could not sleep on his back. The cane which was the only second protection tool at home after a lathi & was thrown out of the house. Father knew tough-minded his son is. After this incident, he never asked Benson to amend his ways. Not that Benson was totally out of control and an alcoholic or a chain smoker but had the determination to look strong & fearless.

Benson at heart was quite soft, a caring human being with empathy, ready to extend all possible help to others. He knew that somehow, he has to now get employed and move ahead in life. A government job was sought-after job those days and the route to a government job was sports. While doing his Inter- college he started playing in a sports stadium with friends and soon got acknowledged as a fine player though disabled. The coach spotted him, trained him and got an opportunity to play at the State level.

It was a marvel to see him play table tennis. Everyone would become astonished, pleasantly surprised to see his game. At the State level, he ended up becoming a runner-up to the champion stood second winner. What followed was little limelight in terms of a few interviews in local dailies & local radio stations. His ENOUGH was to get a government job through this route. He got one in the UP government at the tehsil level.

Why it did not occur to him that making a career in sports would have probably brought him to the National level? He could have included becoming a National player in his ENOUGH! Why was he not able to dream more? Why someone was not able to coach him and encourage him to pursue athletics and show him his future opportunities? Were there no examples of achievement like this to draw inspiration from? Wish there were.

Every life has its own unique set of obstacles, failures, and accomplishments, which is why it's critical to search for local success stories. When there aren't enough people telling you about your potential, you often find someone close to you to be an inspiration.

He achieved his ENOUGH, and landed a government job, what next? Of course, marriage and a family are the way society goes on and on. It is so important to keep defining ENOUGH at every stage of life to continue to making progress. He got posted at a remote location & would be free by 5:30 pm. No sports facility to further sharpen his play. Away from family & a bachelor with only a TV set & radio to the pass time. Being in different locations, meeting family was once in a while, mostly it was postcards and occasional trunk calls to link up with parents and siblings. It was like a loin in the wild with nothing to hunt! He required some actions to kill time rather than use it productively.

Neighbors get together at a card table with booze became a routine. They were all married & had children but he was a loner. Their first priority was family and the second was passing time with entertainment through cards and limited booze.

His priority was to while away time till he gets up the next day. It was a dead small kasba/town, with nothing for entertainment. The nearest city was approx. 35 km away and the highway was always risky to drive a two-wheeler. So, mostly he got confined to this dead kasbah or town.

Though he became a drunkard & a frequent gambler losing and winning sometimes, he did not lose his kindness, care and empathy & remained a good human being. He was aware that in the long run, a normal girl without any physical disability may not remain happy in marriage with him. So, he advised parents to look for a girl who has some weaknesses and was from a middle-class or poor family.

His wife was a fair beautiful lady with the only challenge of quite a blurry vision & she would recognize people by their footstep sound and off-course voice. Her real aunt did not have any babies and was divorcee. Aunt raised her from childhood in a beautiful hill station. She was a graduate and competent at all household chores. She cooked so well and tasty food that it was difficult to stop eating.

While she practically could not see, she did all domestic chores perfectly by arranging everything in order, her home remained clean all the time. She did use all kitchen gadgets like a stove, gas, heater & mixer etc. She was a perfect life partner material.

They got blessed with a boy. He was a healthy and absolutely normal baby. She wanted a good future for him & always insisted Benson arrange good education and proper upbringing for him. The environment in that small town was not at all conducive for children grooming. This was a major point of contention between the couple perhaps the only point of dissatisfaction of his wife.

Benson was not able to get rid of boozing, his mind body & soul were so accustomed to it that they rejected all efforts. He was in a swamp struggling to come out but was getting stuck further deep. He was conscious of ills but a stage of helplessness had come probably it was too late then to try getting rid of boozing.

His son was growing up watching his father drinking, getting drunk. Every child idolizes his father & this daily scene at home became normal for his son. The entire family life was in shambles. Any extent of counselling by the family was rendered useless. Darkness was inevitable, she had an argument wherein she said that it was beyond her scope now to fight for the good future of her son. She went to bed never to wake up again. Till her last breath she took complete care of Benson & her son, the only grudge was his drinking habit. She lost this battle to pull up her husband from the swamp.

When one of your plane's engines fails, all of your efforts are focused on trying to salvage what you can. Benson's mother started living with them. Nothing in their lives altered. Instead of trying to stop him from drinking, she concentrated on her grandson's upbringing. The son was also very devoted to Benson and was always willing to lend a hand. It was little angel parenting his father rather than father raising him.

The mother & Benson both lost the battle of life. Benson's soul surely was not at peace while leaving for the heavenly abode. He probably expected much more support from his brothers than was given. There is this Hindu ritual of hanging a pitcher filled with water on a tree for the departed soul to quench their thirst. The departed soul remain on the earth for 13 days. After so many tries the pitcher did not hang on the tree and water kept falling. Ultimately it was then kept at tree roots.

It is so important to define 'ENOUGH' so that there is no unfulfilled desire left while calling it a day in this World. His son was then brought up by his real uncle, the grown-up even to the elders of the family. Benson was in a government job and his son got a substitution after completing the intermediate.

'History repeats itself' is an old adage. Son played cricket at the State level & was very active till he started boozing. All his uncles and aunts counselled him & gave the example of his father's destroyed life. But nothing impacted him, maybe because as per his earliest memory of his father, he believed it to be absolutely normal.

The traditional solution which a family always comes up with is 'the marriage' with a belief that after marriage and kids, things shall improve. While this belief & solution did not work for his father, the family had no other clue.

The girl's widow mother knowing the boozing habits of the boy, agreed to the marriage. She could have declined this offer since there was no financial crisis with her and her daughter was working in government. But as it was destined. A daughter was born from this wedlock. Boozing lead to heart failure with an end to another misfired life. Who is to be blamed for such a waste of lives?

It is so important for each to define ENOUGH at every stage of life & keep defining upon reaching each milestone for the next one & so on. Always there must be been some dream to look up to and work for it. That's what life is all about. It's like cycling, one has to keep pedaling, keep balancing, and keep bringing it back on the right track, keep looking ahead to avoid a fall.

She the Hustler

Nailah, the eldest of all sibling was a cute girl grown into a fair, beautiful lady with attractive features. It was a period where age expectancy was around 25 years & families used to be large having seven – eight children so that few can survive if parent's luck turns out to be bad. Though, it was a deep-rooted mindset to be happier with the birth of Boys over Girls.

"Ghar Lakshmi aaee hei" was more of a consolation rather than actually welcoming Goddess Lakshmi in the true sense. Though contradictory since everyone would pray to Goddess Lakshmi for money & prosperity but would use her name as a consolation on the birth of a girl child. What if people actually welcome a girl child as Goddess Lakshmi? Would there ever be a need to pray for her since she is already present in the form of a daughter, a sister, or a mother?

Doha-

"जाकी रही भावना जैसी, प्रभु मूरत देखी तिन तैसी।"

Meaning in Hindi-

"राम चरितमानस के बालकांड की इस चौपाई का अर्थ हैं- जिसकी जैसी भावना होती है, उसे उसी रूप में भगवान दिखते है।"

Roman English-

"JAKI RAHI BHAVANA JAISI, PRABHU MOORAT TIN DEKHI WAISI."

Meaning in English-

"In whichever way one chooses to perceive Lord, in that very form the Lord appears to him".

The first kid provides delight and joy to the parents, whether it is a boy or a girl. This is especially true in blended households with grandparents, uncles, aunts, and cousins. Because they were hesitant to show their affection for their children in front of their parents, several fathers in those days used to covertly cuddle their kids.

But daughters have always had their plusses. A beautiful-hearted person Nailah became a friend to her mother & to her youngest sister despite an age gap of two decades. Being the eldest Nailah did help her mother to bring up younger siblings. Daughters are no less than Sons in any way & this mindset which creates a differentiation that must be made redundant. She saw the birth of six siblings until the youngest started sleeping in the middle of his parents & becoming stubborn not to sleep anywhere else. Population control measures were not so common in small towns and neither there was emergent awareness to control it.

Nailah was growing up in a joint family consisting of six sub-families with grandparents, uncles, aunts & cousins learning about life's gives & takes, favoritism, real affection and the artificial one, affluence, abundance with a subfamily & lesser fortune with other and some being destitute. The status of subfamily within a joint family depends upon the capabilities & actions of its head.

It is only human to be biased which gets reflected thru servings to own children and nephews/ nieces further bias comes on basis of financial status amongst nephews/nieces. Sometimes this bias goes unnoticed, sometimes it is ignorable and sometimes it is quite visible but it exists. This bias gives self-realization to a child about ways of life. This bias gets automatically developed even amongst real brothers- sisters which gets reflected in simple acts and its human nature and natural as the adage goes – all five fingers can never be the same. The weakest or perceived weak is the most sufferer of such a bias.

Sometimes virtues like humility & respect are taken as weaknesses. Very few can differentiate between a bow as a mark of respect & a bow laced with greed or expectation or appeasement. One must be expressive. It is important to tell a person what you mean & desire.

'NO' is an important word as it saves one from many difficulties. No need to share your actual position thinking that the other person shall sympathize and offer help rather a distance gets created. 'Haves' always have this fear that 'Have-nots' have an eye on their wealth despite any relationship between the two.

As the idiom goes "Band Mutthi Lakh Ki, Khuli to Khaak ki." बंद मुट्ठी लाख की खुल गई तो खाक की" -भेद नहीं खुलने पर इज्जत बनी रहती है.

Let people keep guessing & they would behave appropriately. A joint family has always been the best training ground for any child to face the real world outside. There are Givers, Takers & Equalizers. Nailah's experiences stemming out of joint family living made her believe that being an Equalizer is the right approach to life. Tit for Tat mindset.

She got groomed as iron-willed having the nerve of steel & being a hustler. She saw all faces of the life of affluent cousins, low & middle-income class cousins all in a single joint family. This did help her form her ambitions about how she wanted to shape her life not knowing that her life was to be tortuous but the twist shall come so early!

She was just about twelve years of age, a blessed childhood with all happiness, running around, playing, dancing, studying & having bliss. She & her younger sister danced well. Someone may wonder how they learned dance steps without YouTube, 24X7 TVs etc. being there. Today there are multiple easily accessible options to learn dance steps. About Seventy-five - Eighty years ago how they learned beautiful dancing in rhythm? One day while dancing to a song being aired on the radio, she suddenly fell down & could not get up. Her left knee gave way.

Doctors, Homeopaths, Hakims & Vaidya – the Ayurveda practitioner were all consulted at different times but the problem could not be diagnosed. Medical Science was still evolving. She was not able to bend her leg below the knee. Fortunately, her leg could take the load of her body and did not stop developing.

A sudden break to life at twelve years was a rude shock life gave to her. In adolescence age she learned to walk without support and come to terms with this disability of a lifetime. She could not walk fast what to think of running. Her disability to walk normally was quite evident in the way she walked. She was a hustler and never wanted to have sympathy & pity from others. She decided to fight it out instead of getting into despondency.

Today, medical science knows the reasons for this disability, which is totally curable with many possible treatments. This condition is called a "locked knee". This means knee can't be straighten or bent. It can be a very painful condition that limits not only the knee's range of motion—the degree to which the joint can move—but your ability to walk, step up, or even sit down comfortably. This locked knee can happen due to a condition like a meniscus tear that may be physically preventing the knee from moving, or a case of tendonitis causes so much pain that the knee cannot bend or extend normally. Often, the cause of a truly locked knee is a so-called "bucket handle" meniscus tear. With this, a large fragment of the torn cartilage in the knee (called the meniscus) can become wedged/forced within the joint, preventing normal movement.

Left untreated, a meniscus tear can limit your daily life and ability to participate in exercise and sports. In serious cases, it can develop into long-term knee problems, like arthritis. Today this condition can be treated through surgery.

Sadly, knowledge of the cause & treatment wasn't known Seventy-five - Eighty years back in India. During the

1960s arthroscopic surgery started successfully in Japan & Europe. However, the first meniscus tear was described in the year 1731.

Adolescence age is the best period of life when a child transits into being an adult. This is the formative period when a person starts defining what and how future life would be led; the dreams, the infatuations, the attraction, the ambition, the career, the aim & goals etc. all start to get defined. High School to Intercollege/Senior Secondary to College – graduation and post-graduation get planned. This hasn't changed for ages.

The beginning of the four ashrams/stages of life is as defined Brahmacharya (student), Grhastha (householder), Vanaprastha (forest walker/forest dweller), and Sannyasa (renunciate). In the contemporary world, no one seems to follow the last two- Vanaprastha & Sannyasa. We remain clung to the life of Grhastha jeevan, first our own children and then their children with a hope to see grand children's children.

Nailah had her decisions & choices to make. To become despondent, dependent on the pity of others or to become self-reliant & lead an independent life with pride. It was a period when parents and society as whole expected and deemed it fit to marry girls at an early age. If not early, after they got educated but working girl was not so common, especially in small towns & cities. Fortunately, her parents were ahead of their times and were open for her to lead life the way she wanted. They respected her decisions and choices. Nailah chose to hustle it out and stand on her own & making her capable of leading a dignified life.

She did not choose an easy route to marry a caring person & live on. She instead chose to be self-reliant and build her career. She decided to remain a bachelor. It was a tough decision even more challenging with a view to encountering society's viewpoint & outlook during that time, period & environment.

She excluded Marriage from her ENOUGH. Her ENOUGH included a graduation, acquiring some skill set and getting work. The career options were so limited that if any child was asked what he or she wish to become, an Engineer or a Doctor mostly used to be the replies. These were typical answers most parents fed to their child's mind, how many were serious, would only be a guesswork!

She learned & graduated in Music Vocal and wanted to sing on Akashvani – the local city radio station though she worked for some time as an Announcer- RJ 'radio jockey' as we know today. But soon learned the limitations of this career. Besides a degree in Music Vocal, she did her BA, MA and B Ed. & got inclined to Teaching career.

She had exposure to teaching thru teaching her younger siblings and also the tuition she took to finance her education to some extent. As a teacher, she was a strict teacher to start with and later on learned teaching skills being soft.

She would scold the elder sibling and the younger out of fear shall rattle out all chapters. Elder sibling, of course, rattled out with a scold/slap. ☺. This technique is quite visible on TV shows – a policeman hitting/threatening an accomplice and the main culprit rattling out the truth out of fear of being the next. Poor elder sibling as she had to bear a slap every time but it was good for her as well.

Every year Rakhi, the younger sibling has to doll out compensation for all slaps taken by her with slaps count forgotten.

Nailah with her disability had to really slog out for a career. She got unexpected help from family friends of her father in terms of finding teaching jobs in their cities and also making her part of their family like their own child to work in those cities. She got exposure to the family fabrics of many family friends.

She was growing more experienced in life craft. This exposure made her more flexible, empathetic & mature.

She could understand that simply being strict would not suffice for changing generations, they are looking for a friendlier approach and open family discussions rather than one-sided discussions veiled under respect pretext, the parenting generation then was used to.

Even as teaching experience increased, she had not yet fixed a career. Her younger sister had finally reached marriageable age; therefore, it was time. Since she was adamant that she would not get married, she asked her parents to locate her younger sister a compatible match. Unwillingly, her parents accepted, and family friends recommended a match for her that resulted in a joyful wedding and wedded life.

With the arrival of her younger sister's first female child and the start of the third generation, Nailah swiftly acquired the title "Mousi." Nailah's quest for a stable career was continuing and finally, an unexpected help knocked on the door to pave the way for a government job as a Teacher for junior & senior secondary classes. The period started when she could earn more than her expenses.

Parents were getting old, younger siblings had all started their struggle & quest for a career/ life ahead. She learnt about saving money for the future & started subscribing to LIC policies, postal savings, FDs etc. She had her

ENOUGH achieved with a stable career & a position where her future could also be secured.

It was about time for her to define the next ENOUGH for life. Life is like cycling with continuous pedaling required though for a while pedaling may be stopped to use the momentum generated but to fresh generate momentum need to pedal and keep pedaling.

It's only human to be in a company, to care & love, be cared & loved, share the happiness, joys & sorrows of the daily grind. It's extremely difficult to live a loner, it's like being alone in a crowd. It was in adolescence that she decided not to marry as she thought it would impede her quest for self-dependence. Now she was a mature, well-groomed, chaste, confident woman and decided to get into the institution of marriage, to bring up a family & seek happiness, joy & peace in doing so.

It was a much reliving decision for her parents, brothers & sisters. A moment of joy for all. Happiness is nothing but a collection of tiny moments which have brought laughter, smile, relief and peace to life.

It was quite an event to search for a life partner for Nailah. She was above the age norm & with this walking challenge. There are people who always want to take advantage of situations. The Grownup even to the elders – the chaperone and his friends scrutinized & investigated thoroughly all proposals which came in response to a matrimonial advertisement.

It was shocking to learn that people who were already married or had two wives already, gamblers etc. sent the proposal. Had it not been efforts of this 'Grownup even to the elders – the chaperone, her life would have been in a mess.

Finally, a suitable match was found and the marriage took place. Thereafter it was a blissful 10-11 years with children being born, life sailed through smooth & rough terrains with daily grind till the day when her husband got hospitalized and never returned back.

She was shattered and once again had to face the toughest face of life. Soon she gathered herself. God manifests in many ways, when this tragedy occurred, the Grownup even to the elders- the chaperone, did not wait for a single day and brought them to his home. God would always extend a hand through someone.

We all have experienced such manifestation of GOD in our lives so many times when it was direly needed. HE MANIFESTS for sure. Those whom HE chose for extending support are the lucky ones. Therefore, never ever miss an opportunity to help someone in need, maybe this time GOD has chosen you to manifest HIMSELF.

Nailah again had to decide the ENOUGH. Her husband did not leave fortunes being in business which did not flourish so well! But was sufficient to run the family decently and with dignity. Her income as a teacher was put into savings. Mutual Funds got added to her savings instrument bouquet. She did build financial security continuously with this saving habit and still living decently but without an extravaganza.

Her focus was to educate her children and make them a fighter & a hustler ready to face any challenges that life may throw at them. She did succeed and both shined in life. They love their mother for the way she brought them up and the teachings they got. Nailah is not fazed by past happenings and lives in the present moment relishing the bliss of lives every breath that she takes. She isn't bothered about what is next. There is financial freedom attained through systematic investments, pensions etc., and has all facilities, and lifestyles which money can buy. Her ENOUGH now is to enjoy every moment of it.

This story spans about five generations from Nailah's grandparents to her grandchildren, close to 100 years of understanding the changing World, values and lifestyles. Yet the struggle of life remains to be same and the only solution is to keep pedaling till one call it a day in this World.

The choice to be happy lies in one's hand, no one else can decide. It is so important to manage expectations, and clearly define what is ENOUGH. So that once achieved there is satisfaction, happiness, and joy to move on to the next ENOUGH level.

ENOUGH is just about a stage of nothing more and nothing less than required to move on & live the desired life. It is a position which gives satisfaction on outcomes of all efforts, toils, hustling, hurting, falling, rising & running again.

The Beauty Parlour

The Beauty Parlour has many symbolic messages for a life to live better. In difficult times these symbolic steps are necessary to be taken as self-help in coming out of a difficult time. Simply put it is a place where people go to enhance their physical appearance. Here are few symbols of efforts for a better life.

Self-care:

Visiting a beauty parlour involves taking time out of your busy schedule to prioritize self-care. This act of self-care can be seen as a reminder that taking care of yourself is important and can help you lead a better life. It shows that you value yourself enough to take care of your physical and emotional needs.

Confidence Quotient:

A visit to a beauty parlour can boost confidence, and self-esteem & enhance the confidence quotient. When you feel good about yourself, you are more likely to take on challenges and pursue your goals with confidence and determination.

Personal grooming:

A beauty salon can be viewed as a representation of good hygiene and personal grooming. Maintaining one's look is a sign of respect for oneself. Personal grooming can eventually result in a better life through enhancing social and professional connections.

Positive change:

A beauty parlour can also symbol to positive changes in life. One can experiment with new hairstyles, makeup looks, and skincare routines that can help feel refreshed and renewed. This positive change can inspire you to make other positive changes in life, such as adopting a healthier lifestyle or pursuing a new career or adopting a renewed positive attitude.

Taking Care:

Furthermore, beauty parlours provide a relaxing and soothing environment that can help reduce stress and anxiety. When you take time for yourself to get pampered and cared for, it can have a positive impact on your mental and emotional well-being. The feeling of being taken care of and looking your best can make you feel more confident and readier to take on the world.

Self-care, confidence, overall personal grooming, making good life adjustments, and taking care of oneself and others around oneself are some of the important behaviors and qualities that contribute to contentment, happiness, and peaceful living.

By doing these things, you can get through any obstacles. Kara was at the cusp of deciding about her career having a kid, a loving husband, ageing father & mother in law. She lived in a small city where growth opportunities were quite bleak & almost negligible. They had a house where a room with a separate entrance could be spared. Be it a small city or a big city, women love to look beautiful and that's where next-door beauty parlours come in handy.

Sensing an opportunity in this self-employed business, Kara completed a beautician course and set out to start a beauty parlour. Her USP was the use of branded beauty products with a reasonable fee & personal care. She did not charge extra for branded products and instead negotiated better discounts from wholesalers. Branded products instilled confidence & reasonable fee gave a value for money & her personal care gave smiles to customers. Soon she became a known name in the vicinity.

That's what Kara was looking at. Her ENOUGH was to reach a point of a reasonable income thru good customer care in the available time at her disposal after taking care of her family.

Her next ENOUGH was to give good education to her kid and also build war-chest for their marriage & own future.

Her life has not been as straight as it looks now. It had its own share of lows but then she adopted virtues of Self-care, created Self Confidence quotient, carried out Personal grooming over all, brought positive thinking & changes in life & took her care by being empathetic with self and everyone around which lead to the present-day position – a step towards peaceful life ahead & becoming ready for all future challenges that life shall throw at her.

Kara was born to a middle-class parent, father being in government service. His posting was in a small town at a remote location without basic facilities like good schools & thus no good company for a decent upbringing of children. There is this saying that 'Ek To Kadvaa Kareela Woh Bhi Neem Chadda', one of the poor town infrastructures and added on top of the kid's misery was his boozing habits.

Their whole life was disturbed and in shambles. Evils of a drunkard father are well known & so much publicized, what to mention here, one can déjà vu these. But their mother taught them to respect their father and take care.

It was like a daily family sequel that both parents would argue, and end up quarreling over mother's concern for their kid's proper upbringing. They had just begun attending primary school that with in flash of a second their mother lost battle for their good upbringing.

The following morning, she did not awaken with all of her daily arguments put to rest. Even after working hours, her father had trouble caring for himself, let alone the kids. Life was somehow stumbling along with no sign of normality. A lever failure caused by excessive drinking had a foreseeable result, and their father also disappeared suddenly from their lives.

The neighbors appealed with the District Magistrate to let both children live in the same public housing unit until her brother grows up and finds a job to replace his father's, since the pension will help them get by until then. Not knowing about their relatives, the District Magistrate consented to do so for humanitarian reasons.

To provide desperately needed assistance, God appoints a chaperone in every family. One was given to both kids. They were taken home by their uncle and aunt to be cared after like their own children. They had two of their own already.

Kara's aunt was a strict disciplinarian, who believed in tough love. She was determined to see her sons succeed in life, and she treated Kara no differently. Kara was expected to work hard, study diligently, and do well in school. Her aunt's strict parenting style meant that Kara had a limited social life.

She spent most of her time helping with chores around the house & studying. While she often in heart resented her aunt's strict ways, Kara also knew that her aunt cared for her deeply and wanted the best for her. Kara was not bright in her studies no matter how hard she tried.

Kara's childhood was a painful one. She missed her parents deeply and struggled to fit into her new family. While she had better comfort and dignified life but her aunt's strict ways often left her feeling isolated and alone. Her aunt was a softer person from inside but maintained a tough stance for benefit of children.

However, despite the hardships, Kara remained determined to succeed in life. She worked hard in school to carry forward her studies. She went on to live with her elder brother who by the time had completed his studies till intermediate and got a government job in lieu of their father. Kara did complete her graduation during this time while taking care of all the house works & cooking etc.

Fortunately, the posting was in a proper city where many relatives lived. Which gave psychological and physical protection to both kids. Kara's life taught many lessons to her. She came to know what the right approach is and what is wrong. How she has to lead her life. She observed happily families of relatives around and got to know family values, the learnings she had missed in her childhood. She understood the value of being financially independent. While she was a kid, her father's pension & lump sum amount received after death were there to support them.

Uncle kept the pension and lump sum amount safely invested for their future needs like marriage etc. She had started to think about her way of life where her kids shall not have to go through the pains and traumas. She put in all efforts to equip herself with the capabilities to live in a dignified way. Dreams, Ambitions, Hope & Efforts are what keep this Universe so vibrant, dynamic and going. She was growing up and had her uncle & aunt worried about marriage.

It was one summer that she visited her maternal aunt's house to stay for few days. There she met the next-door boy. It is still a good habit in small towns and cities that neighbor take out time to meet each other and become family friends. A casual conversation to know each other led to revelations of life's trials and unpleasant journeys. Both had their own share of grief, sorrows faced thus far.

The discussions became frequent even beyond this visit and bonding began to surface. What started as sympathy lead to empathy, to the feeling of being on the same platform, to sharing a common dream, to infatuation, to liking & finally led to a decision of living together.

It was the turn of the elders to meet and finalize the relationship. Both uncles of Kara met their counterparts. It was a repeat scene from the Bollywood super famous film Sholay 1975 wherein Jai takes the proposal of Viru to Basanti's mousi and gradually reveals all ills of Viru in a fun way.

Initially, it was not clear if both the uncles wanted this relationship to be fixed or otherwise since all negative aspects of Kara's life were shared openly with the boy's elders. But that was the right thing to do so that the boy side knew everything which may have spoiled this relationship after marriage. Actually, this open sharing increased the confidence of the boys' family since they were already having information about past events in Kara's Life because she had told herself.

It was time that Kara got to again enjoy a family. Her husband was quite caring and so were his step-parents. The family grew with Kara giving birth to kid. While earnings were never surplus neither there was any challenge in a decent life. They both were doing all efforts for a good future. There was no room for any complaint by Kara as she was much better off than before being loved, taking and giving care of family, and seeding good values amongst her kid. While being thankful about what she had, they are working harder with more effort to secure a better future. Opening the Beauty Parlour is one such step towards their next ENOUGH.

Ainth (ऐंठ) - Not Less Than Any

Keegan was quite a handsome man around his town. Curly black thick hairs, fair skin, broad forehead, six feet one-inch height, thin built and beautiful features. He had low & throaty deep voice with a deep sound coming from deep down in throat like that of a visionary, soothing & serious. Mostly he would keep a trim Stache moustache that sits just above the lips. His looks would become more versatile. He obviously attracted awe and envy amongst a group of young guys around his home in the mohalla.

The young men circle in Mohalla was all rich and had a blessed life except for Keegan. Keegan got his place in inner circle due to his magnanimous personality. They were graduating together with some very brilliant and some average. For most young lads to become a graduate was ENOUGH. Since there were not too many career options but that did not mean young lads did not become engineers, doctors and lawyers though it is true that only most brilliant and lucky ones could go for prestigious, respected and dreamt professions like these. Government Jobs then also were an attraction considered to be secure & respectful. Family business was always the next choice if it existed.

Keegan's father had inherited a farm land, couple of houses including the one in this ancestral mohalla. His mother always felt that during division of wealth they did not get equal share & clearly voiced her dissent while division of money lender's wealth was being carried out by his eldest son & daughter.

Keegan's grandfather the money lender had huge wealth. It was said that he had pile of 'silver bricks' kept in a basement where entry was prohibited. Later this basement was used to store grains to be finally closed permanently as the generations changed. It was a big joint family till grandparents were alive without any shortages. Even if a son is not earning, he would still be married, have children and everyone would have sufficient to live jointly. Even if one person earned was ENOUGH. Happiness existed then also.

The prosperity of grandparents & great-grandparents transcended in the form of pride, ego, and some kind of arrogance and it can be aptly described as Ainth (ਐਂਠ).

There is this proverb in Hindi – Rassi Jal Gayee Par Bal Nahi Gaye'. It can be said that the princely or royal privileges of being rich are lost but not the swag, ego, bluster & sense of entitlement remains. The feeling or an attitude of being 'Not Less than Any' remains.

This feeling or attitude is at times such an important feeling, a sentiment that can save from the traps of an inferiority complex and depression. This Ainth (ਐਂਠ) acts as a kick, a motivation to keep putting efforts to prove in society. While this Ainth (ਐਂਠ) sometime may become a ridiculed but still it is a big motivation to keep going on with a head high.

Keegan's father got into farming not out of a choice but had no other choice. Rental from inherited houses was another income source from tenants who were once the owners & lost their ownership due to loans taken from the money lender. They did not vacate or increased the rent. Most houses were sold back to them for peanuts since money was a constant need.

Keegan had five younger sisters and all had to be educated to live a decent life ahead. Having a big family was not a taboo than in the 1940s & 1950s. People were not bothered about having more children, one because of the low rate of survival and second joint family living & thirdly no one talked about long-term socio-financial impact. Ayushman Khurana, Neena Gupta & Gajraj Rao starred 2018 Bollywood Drama / Comedy movie – 'Badhai Ho' may be an awkward thing to happen now but in those times, it was a common occurrence. Sometimes the age gap between the eldest and youngest siblings is 20-25 years.

No, guess that soon Keegan had to act as chaperone to his family with ailing parents, growing up sisters. Farmland sold, inherited houses sold while few of inherited ornaments remaining & those were kept for daughter's marriages. A Start from the Zero. A hell of a life ahead which can send shivers across anyone's spine at the mere thought of it.

There he was in the midst of it with no idea where to go. Yet he had his Ainth (ऐंठ), the 'not less than any' attitude that lead to a strong will to prove to himself, to his pals & to close relatives by coming out of troubled times with flying colors & build a future.

Keegan had to define what shall be ENOUGH to move on. Of course, an income level which would make two times a day meal feasible. Then there were responsibilities of sisters to be settled in a respectable way. He did not ask for money from any friend or relative & frankly no one even offered to help monetarily despite most of them being financially quite well placed. Though he did odd jobs in between to keep the stove burning he was looking for a work opportunity with achievement-linked incentives earning beyond a limited fixed salary. Because his ENOUGH required to have more income than two times a day meal requirement.

Proverbs are made out of experiences & are actually quite true. There is this one – "A Friend in Need is a Friend Indeed". This implies that most of acquaintance don't stand alongside when one gets into trouble. However, a few who are true friend offer a helping hand.

It is through such incidents of Unexpected Help that God manifests. Back then banks started a daily deposit scheme to mobilize & increase savings corpus. Daily deposits earned regular interest and was aimed at promoting the habit of savings in daily wagers, small shop keepers, small vendors, hawkers etc. while anyone could join this deposit scheme.

To mobilize these deposits banks were appointing agents who would enroll customers for daily deposits. These agents were being offered commissions on these deposits. That would mean the more the deposits, the more the commissions & earnings.

Keegan's friend list had many affluent young lads but all went silent in his troubles except for the one. This one friend had an account with the bank and was friendly with the bank manager. This friend got Keegan appointed as a deposit agent and offered personal guarantee for him which was the basic requirement since deposit agents had to handle cash transactions every day. It was a bold decision on the part of this friend to stand guarantee for Keegan who had nothing except for his zeal and willingness to work hard. What if Keegan would have defaulted?

This is the kind of work Keegan was looking for since he had many miles to cover up and fast. And there was competition since many agents got appointed for this work. The work territories were not defined and kept open to all agents. It was a survival of the fittest scenario. Keegan could not foresee a better opportunity & he burnt all his bridges behind him. No looking back except to make a success out of it.

What followed was a relentless back breaking efforts to increase the daily deposits by Keegan. He would start his day early morning meeting with hawkers who would start their stalls early & this schedule shall go on till evening convincing people about the scheme and collecting daily deposits. Not a day could be missed.

He had no means so he covered the entire route on foot with a bag on his shoulder, a towel on his head to save him from the heat and a bottle of water. It entailed reoccurring visits to the same depositors every day to collect daily deposit installments and make new depositors. So, every day the length of travel increased, and with little money coming in he bought a bicycle, a green color Hero 24 inches.

This became a full 12-hour-a-day work since after coming back home entire collection was to be arranged denomination-wise, entries were to be made for each depositor every day and deposited in the bank the next day. All his sisters and mother helped in currency handling and entry work at home which could not be completed without Keegan's presence though.

Beyond doubt, he left behind many agents who got appointed along with him. His burning desire to lift up his family kept him moving beyond physical limits at times.

What kept him motivated was his Ainth (ਐਂਠ) to not only show people his worth but also to attain a dignified life. The bigger motivation, however, was love for the family. He did not allow people around to feel pity for his family rather they admired him for his determination & hard work. His father again could walk with a high head.

Life is like a bicycle, one has to keep pedaling without resting to maintain a forward movement. There was no stopping for Keegan. To keep pace with time and increase his depositor base he had to increase his mobility. His Family insisted him to buy a scooter or a bike. But he decided to buy a moped which is cheaper, consumed less petrol and could be maneuvered in small streets and congested markets.

The handsome boy had become a mature, confident man with clear signs of fatigue yet a shining /beaming face with a sense of accomplishment. He ensured that all his sisters completed graduation.

One by one found a suitable match & married them. He actually kept a promise of protection to the sisters which every year a brother gives to sisters while they tie rakhi thread on the wrist of their brothers – "Rakhi ke bandhan ko nibhana".

For his future, he had also started to invest by keeping his ENOUGH within reach. These long-term consistent savings are compounded to give the desired financial security. He is contended & a satisfied man with no dependence on anyone. He has his time and spends it the way he wishes.

The Unwilling Salesman

Make your passion a profession; do what you love to do & not what you don't like.... many such sermons/advises float around entire social media. Fact is not many are able to do that or get an opportunity to do that. It is something like everyone wish to fall in love before marriage but mostly couple's fall in love after their marriage & make a success out of it.

A love marriage at times appears to be the outcome of the availability of a boy & a girl at a common place & time both not having any direct or indirect family relation near or distant. Had they not met, how an affair would start? Can you plan a love affair or it just happens? Likewise, most people fall in love with their work after taking it up. The challenge is to adapt to it & the art is to make a success out of it.

The Narrator shared a story about a salesperson who had no choice but to become a salesman. With due regards & apologies to Sales Profession, it is surely not the first choice of many. Sometimes it is the only choice. But it is a big life savior for many who otherwise have not been ready & suitable for other professions.

The fact of life is that everyone is selling. If you are a teacher then you are selling your teaching skills of making subjects easy to understand in turn to attract more students, if you are a doctor or an advocate then you are selling confidence by convincing & showing people your expertise so that they come back again and do a referral for you, so on and so forth. Look around & you will find that everyone is selling.

Sales is actually a way to successful life as it develops your personality in many ways. Let's know this through a backronym of SALES & what requires to be a successful salesperson and a successful person

Letter S stands for 'Self-confidence'; letter A stands for 'Appearance' both physical grooming & Inner appearance which is the Intent like trustworthiness, reliability, caring etc.; letter L stands for 'listening', not just hearing but actual ability to understand the unsaid, letter E stands for 'Enthusiasm' being enthusiastic about whatever has to be done & the last letter S stands for 'Service', being helpful and a friend in need.

These qualities/ personality attributes/traits can be developed & acquired by design. These do not come from genes/ by birth as a default. Everyone can acquire these personality attributes for a taste of success, these are not just a need for sales professionals alone.

This guy Saylor was a salesman forced/compelled by the situation. He was the seventh of seven siblings. It is a blessing to be the youngest one. The bowl of life remains filled with protection, love, care & joy. So many grownups to become your chaperone at different junctures of life. His childhood was quite blessed with all luxuries around. Living in a bungalow, moving to a grander house with so many rooms and a joint family having grandparents & so many uncles, aunts and cousins. Then there was a period when his family faced a financial crunch and he faced difficulties in life. He experienced both the ENOUGH & barely enough/ shortages early in life.

He also saw his mother coping with shortages and managing life ensuring that her children don't feel lesser & low down. His parent's behavior during ENOUGH times was such that even during shortages time all friends and relatives gave equal respect to the family and extended full support in whatever way they could. His mother always taught them the importance of deeds, honesty, humility, care, self-respect, ingenuity, resilience, faith & gratitude to them. She demonstrated that through her acts all the time even when she had less than needed.

These values always brought respect to all of this family even after parents were gone.

All these realizations happened to Saylor much later in life when he began to understand life and started to relate what his mother told and how she acted upon. He could understand the value of the experiences he has gone through in his innocence age.

His childhood was that of an aimless wanderer. Even if he tried he was not able to understand the lessons & was average at his studies and remained so. The good thing that happened to him was his family moved to the big city. Otherwise, in that small town, he had no career. His only aim was to become a graduate and find a job.

Parents were worried about what would happen to Saylor but believed in positive outcomes. They had a firm belief in God's Will that has always manifested to help them at the most difficult sections of their life. Thus, they did not express their worry.

There are times that alter the path of everyone's life. It took place when Saylor's father became bedridden owing to high blood pressure. He was able to move, but only with assistance. Saylor was the only one who could join his father to meetings because he was finishing off his senior secondary education before going to college. These interactions with his father and seeing his social group provided Saylor a glimpse into what life is like, and his desires for a respectable living began to take hold. He became aware and committed to his career.

Academically, it was too late to do anything more because he had to start working right away and couldn't afford to continue his studies. He had his choices to make.

He had begun learning English because he understood that communication is a crucial skill in life and that without it, there would be no chance of success. Reading aloud to his father while recording word definitions helped him learn English the fastest. This also increased his vocabulary. At first, it seemed as though he had to consult the dictionary several times for each phrase to comprehend the meaning of the words. However, efforts started to bear fruit, and used a dictionary less frequently.

This enhanced his communication and spoken English. Honesty, dedication, integrity, loyalty, were like the trademark his parents had earned over time for their family and basis this one of his father's friends wanted to kind of adopt Saylor as a confidant disciple/assistant. This was one choice wherein right from with world go, Saylor would have been rolling in money. But soon Saylor realized that it would be like becoming a traffic policeman surrounded by many cars but none of his. Most importantly, serving an individual has its own risks, when it would turn to slavery, no one can predict. In fact, even many promoters treat their employees as slaves even today.

Upon graduating Saylor's father arranged a recommendation for a Job. The interview took place & since it was a reference of the owner of the brand, the Vice President had to offer some job. So, the offer was a clerk position in the warehouse at the Kashipur plant of that company. The pay offered was Rs.700/- per month and a free room at the factory in worker's quarters. Saylor did not accept this offer nor did his father force him to do so.

The first job picked up thru classified vacancy column of the Hindustan Times newspaper was a salesman to sell the Annual Edition of an Indian travel book on the lines of Discovery India – the Air India Magazine to tour agencies and even individuals. This was a daily wage job at Rs.30/- a day plus 10% commission i.e. Rs.18/- per annual edition sold. The Boss Mr. Srinivasan was a compassionate person and wanted to give a chance to a young boy to start a career against the wish of the circulation manager.

As luck would have been, he passed away at the early age of 40 years due to a heart attack leaving behind a wife and a boy. The next thing was that the circulation manager asked Saylor to leave since the company did not wish to pursue the idea of Mr. Srinivasan. However, during this one month, some 23 books were sold by Saylor. Alongside visiting tour organizers in CP for sale, he did door-to-door sales to rich people and they bought for their interest towards such picturesque edition and more so to encourage this young boy.

This way journey of an Unwilling Sales person started. It was around the same time that Eureka Forbes' classified advertisement for Salesman Vacancy was printed. They inducted Saylor for the job of door-to-door – direct sales salesman at a monthly salary of Rs.500/- + Rs.15/- daily allowance and commission slabs.

It was an initial success and a dire need of money for the family that Saylor continued the exhausting job. The first month, Saylor's supervisor accompanied him to show how a sale is made. Out of a total of 14-unit sales, 3 were sold by his supervisor alongside him. It was a training for group leaders and supervisors to lead by example and allow credit of their efforts to be given to their team trainees. This got a total salary including the commission of Rs.5000/- to Saylor.

The task was really difficult; it was virtually on par with that of a laborer. Carrying a demonstration unit in a 24" hard case door to door to demonstrate and try to sell. Only a few demonstrations resulted in sales; the most did not. At 7 a.m., the daily ritual would begin by getting to the meeting place. From there, it was office time and evening again around 5 pm meeting point and then field. From there, it was going to assigned territory, knocking on doors for appointments and demos with a break in afternoon. There were no holidays; in fact, all holidays were potential days since purchasers would be at home.

His hands had become hard carrying a heavy case. All the pain and exhaustion vanished with a cheque of Rs.5000/- as his first earning. All money was given to Mother who repaid 3 month's overdue ration bill of bania, the shopkeeper. Pride in his mother's eyes became a motivation for Saylor to continue this job.

His Mother asked Saylor to borrow money from his eldest sister and buy a secondhand scooter to help ease physical labor and increase productive field time for more sales. His brother introduced him to savings by taking up a LIC policy assuring that if some month sales are not there, he would pay up the premium. But it was never required.

Saylor defined ENOUGH as a minimum Rs.4000/- per month average income to not only take care of his expenses but also to finance family needs. The entire salary always was handed over to the mother. He could not afford any vices so stayed away from smoking, drinking and expensive non-veg food.

Initially, Saylor's father did not like the work as he was a door-to-door salesman and did not tell his friends but one day after about 6 months Saylor's supervisor visited his home without informing Saylor and convince his father about the company and the job. This must also be part of training supervisors to retain their team of salesmen since the job was so tough and boys left pretty quickly.

Saylor rapidly made a name for himself as a committed, diligent, and goal-oriented worker. Despite having a good grasping power, he attempted to pursue an MBA three times on the recommendation of his brother but never maintained a regular study schedule. But he was always learning, so when he met potential customers in the comfort of their homes with their families to demonstrate a product, he was able to comprehend consumer behavior and decision-making of various customers.

This understanding of consumer behavior gave a sound footing to Saylor in the industry in the later part of his career. The beauty of basic human psychology & behavior is that it does not change over centuries. What St. Kabir Das said some over 600 years ago is still valid, relevant and useful. Or what Vivekananda said is still valid & relevant. Yes, when income class changes so do the needs and corresponding buying behavior.

Saylor's ENOUGH was a steady growth in career & earn respect in society like his father. He knew that he must hone soft skills and keep improving not having hard skills. He read many books on management and started to practice. Some values of a good leader like dedication, delegation, teamwork, credit sharing, and respecting everyone were already learnt by him observing his parents & joint family behavior.

His efforts and work earned the admiration of his seniors, which become a good referral base. All his future assignments and growth came through people who had witnessed his work and knew that he was an asset. Most of the support came as unexpected, where someone referred to his name for the assignments. His soft skills were taking him to places and bringing in growth.

He was a scared guy on the inside who prayed constantly for a wonderful life. His mother advised him to pray for his well-being rather than requesting money from God. She also informed him that no one, not even the wealthiest person, could aid him if God wanted anything terrible, but that if God wanted something good, no one could harm him or stop the goodness. His daily prayers were therefore limited to seeking pardon for any wrongdoing, expressing gratitude for the gifts, clearing obstacles from the way, and upholding honor.

However, not everything was as idyllic as it would have seemed. His life was also tortuous. He was married at a time when his income was just enough to survive. He had ambitions about life and wanted to lead a rich lifestyle which was unthinkable at that time given his resources. This ambition perturbed him from the inside but never created distress. Because he had learned to focus on ENOUGH at a given time, period and environment. He kept his calm, positive outlook & continue to work hard.

He had experienced money getting arranged unexpectedly & none of his work had to suffer for want of it. So, he was sure of God's helping hand but never stopped hustling. It was time for mundan sanskar – head shaving ceremony of both his kids. As per family practice it was to be done at a particular temple near home town with all family members. This would mean quite an expense and he had no savings then. Around the same time, it was announced that he has won a cash incentive for meeting his sales target and he got money.

The mundan sanskar- head shaving ceremony was done in a lavish style inviting all relatives, and offering them lunch and gifts as per rituals. In those days accounting was not that fast since computers had just started being used and tabulation of sales used to take time. Next month it was found out that due to some sale returns, the incentive needs to be recovered by the company. His boss was compassionate and agreed to make EMI of the incentive disbursed.

There were many such instances in his life. One which shook him and his wife was the time of his mother's death. There was practically no money in the home when she passed away. With only Rs10/- at home, his wife served glucose biscuits to her with tea, that's what the last she had asked for.

They were worrying about how money for all rituals shall be arranged. His mother wished that her last rites and rituals must be done without scarcity. There was this call center call from Citibank offering personal loan basis transactions of a credit card. Saylor requested the call center executive about the need that the demand draft called DD needed urgently by the same day evening but the executive promised for next day morning delivery. The DD was delivered. Those days' online transactions were not there. However, once the demand draft is deposited banks used it to en-cash immediately. This enabled Saylor to carry out the last rites and all rituals as per his mother's expectation.

It was unexpected and unknown when Citibank called. How did it occur at that specific moment? Saylor's mother gave her the advice to always pay back loans on time, even if you occasionally need to borrow more money to do so. However, prompt repayment will build credibility.

Saylor used a credit card that allows for interest-free repayment after one month to continue to function. He would make all payments while on tour through a credit card, these tour bills would be uncashed immediately by the company. The money was used for monthly survival, payment of EMIs of home loans and personal loans etc. Money received from the next tour bills was used for credit card payment, this way other than salary one month's tour expenses were rotated. Increments were utilized for extra loans to improve lifestyle.

Alongside, Saylor also saved whatever was feasible without compromising on a basic lifestyle in sync with family & friends circle. Banks always look for such customers who take loans and repay on time therefore, Saylor was the best customer for banks.

There was a long-term benefit of excessive official touring to Saylor. He got an in-depth understanding & the unique nuances of various markets. His relations got better with trade partners. Since he was a frequent traveler, his territory remained free from any unwanted claims arising out of miscommunication or false promises by the sales team. On every visit the accounts were tallied. It was a difficult & manual task than with cheque clearances taking minimum 15 days or even a month for upcountry locations. Professionally this excessive travel benefitted him, he also became commercially sound alongside sales proficient.

One day, Saylor & the quality manager, went on a field visit to a distributor's office to look into any product difficulties. While passing over the pothole, quality manager was unaware of it, his scooter jolted violently. Because of this jerk, Saylor, the pillion rider, had excruciating back agony. He hustled through the discomfort and kept working, but after another four days he was unable to move.

It was determined through testing that the issue is a slip disk. Saylor became utterly immobile and confined on bed. Such are the times when your faith gets tested. His mother came to stay with him and look after him. It was a solace to Saylor, mother having his bedside.

All the worst thoughts crossed his mind leaving him shivering with fear of worse. He prayed for death rather than stay confined to bed and be a burden on his wife. He was fearful as to how she would look after all four kids and him as bedridden? Death would give her some money out of insurance. That money would be used to repay all loans. She is educated and can work to live life ahead.

Doctor R S Sood however gave confidence to Saylor that his condition is not that bad and he shall recover without an operation which had more risk involved. He shared that he treated his wife with the same condition and she is okay. God or Doctor only know the truth but this assurance had a positive impact on Saylor's mind. His mother also made him forcibly repeat the Mahamrityunjaya Mantra which leads to good health.

His faith was restored and started to think of getting well & move on with life. It happened though he had precautions to take. This was a nightmarish period of three months being in bed. Unexpectedly, Saylor's boss supported and allowed his salary plus incentives without any deductions which kept finances running.

His hustling never stopped, due to excessive travel he again had slip disk at the second joint in the spine. Dr. R S Sood came to the rescue and assured him that there is nothing to worry about as he has patients with disc issues at four places in the spine and they are leading a normal life. Of course, life was not normal and Saylor learnt to live with it taking care of movements etc. Dr. R S Sood became Man Friday for Saylor. He recommended Dr. Sood to everyone with any back-related pain issues.

Saylor discovered at one point in his life that if he received Rs.10 lac in a single payment, that would be ENOUGH for next growth. By the time this was set up, the initial 10 lac had grown to 40 lac in order to be ENOUGH, and as time went on and status rose, it eventually led to a loan-free existence.

By being devoted, dependable, a smart worker, upbeat, and adopting a futuristic perspective, he was progressively advancing in his job. Over the course of a 35-year career, he rose to the position of vice president of sales without compromising his integrity, honesty, or ENOUGH.

He consciously did not increase his expenses for a good 12 to 15 years to build a corpus, a war chest for his life ahead. Having ENOUGH to be financially free, it was time to further improve his lifestyle status by moving into a new house in an upwardly mobile locality.

The seeds were sown much earlier for this ENOUGH but Saylor and his family did not know how it would happen and when. During their life journey, they bought two houses which were adjacent to each other with a common wall. After about 15 years the value of these houses increased to a level. Saylor planned to sell one of the houses and invest money further to build a more solid safety net for the future.

Since there was no urgency, Saylor demanded a higher price than prevailing. Finally, one person liked the house and offered the desired price. It got sold. Meanwhile, neighbors got to know that Saylor wish to sell the house. One such neighbor enquired if the house was still available.

It was as if some force guided Saylor to say that one house is sold but the one we stay in is available for sale but at a still higher price. This was not planned though within the family. The neighbor took no chance and paid in advance. So, both houses were sold at a higher than market value.

There was pressure to leave the house for the new owner to shift, and time was quite limited. One option was to move out on rent and continue your search, but rentals were high at the time... One afternoon Saylor got to meet a person while searching the house by way of enquiring with security offices of various societies around. He was a property dealer and offered a flat in the most sought-after new society in the vicinity provided some budget can be increased.

Saylor agreed to see the flat as it was tempting to have a house in this society. Saylor and his family quite liked the flat and its direction which lead to direct sunlight in the entire flat during morning hours with balconies being east facing. The owner of this flat had booked it some eight/nine years earlier and now wanted to sell. Since his stature and ENOUGH increased for still a better house.

The meeting was short and crisp with Saylor clearly stating his budget limit and to the surprise of Saylor and equally, the property dealer, the seller agrees to sell at that price. Later on, the property broker told that the seller had asked for higher value and did not sell at a lower value earlier on two occasions. But why he agreed this time remains a myth.

That's how fate works; the buyers of Saylor's home received what they desired—a well-kept home with good omen—Saylor received what he desired—a posh neighborhood without the need for a loan—and the seller received what he desired—to sell his home to an honest buyer of his choosing at a fair price that would cover the interest portion of his investment.

Everyone received what they deemed to be ENOUGH. Some fifteen years ago Saylor had a colleague. They lost touch afterwards & never connected. One day out of the blue he connected with Saylor.

He had started his own consultancy on Vaastu for corporate houses. They met at Saylor's new house and he checked Vaastu of the house and applied measures to improve positive energies in the house. This was a totally unexpected help. A new house, in high society & full Vaastu compliance. Within a few months, Saylor's only daughter got married. Sons were already pursuing their career.

It was time that Saylor had to define the next ENOUGH.

Conclusion: Peace @ Enough

Asking what is ENOUGH is an important question. Everyone must ask this at some point of their lives. The ENOUGH may vary for each individual since each have their own set of desires, wants, aspirations, abilities and capabilities. There is no one-size-fits-all approach to determining ENOUGH. Goals, priorities, and circumstances will all play a key role in determining ENOUGH.

Many individuals find it challenging to decide what is ENOUGH. Finding the right balance between a Want and a Need may be quite difficult. However, in order to live a full life and prevent unneeded tension and worry, one must define what ENOUGH is.

The idea of "enough" refers to the point at which someone would feel comfortable and pleased after having met their fundamental wants and desires.

There is no place for greed in defining ENOUGH. If there is greed then nothing can ever be enough. Greed & Peace don't co-exist. Attaining the ENOUGH leads to Peace though. It is a path to attaining Peace & contentment. Peace leads to Happiness. How can a person be happy if he or she is not having a peaceful mind?

Deciding what is ENOUGH requires a deep understanding of one's own values, priorities, and goals. It involves reflecting on what truly matters in life and what one is willing to sacrifice to achieve their desired level of contentment. For some, enough may mean financial stability, a fulfilling career, or a strong support network of family and friends or survival at that point in time. For others, it may mean a simple life with minimal possessions, meaningful relationships, or a focus on personal growth and development.

Financial security is a crucial consideration when choosing whether enough is enough. It's important to be aware of your spending patterns. This entails taking a deeper look at money and figuring out how much is required to pay for necessities like clothes, housing, food, health care, and transportation, among others. How investing a percentage of the available cash to savings might lead to financial security or independence. Choosing the amount that would be "ENOUGH" to meet future needs really requires redefining necessities to a level that is just about appropriate to live a normal/acceptable existence.

Once individuals have identified their priorities and goals, they can then work to develop a plan to achieve them. This may involve setting realistic and achievable goals, creating a budget, developing a savings plan, and making decisions about how they spend their time and resources.

It is important to note that deciding what is enough is a process that can change over time. As individuals grow and evolve, their priorities and requirements may shift, and what was once ENOUGH may no longer be sufficient. Therefore, it is important to regularly reevaluate one's ENOUGH and priorities and adjust accordingly.

Deciding the ENOUGH also involves making peace with what one already has. Practicing gratitude can help us appreciate what we have and recognize when we have enough. Take time each day to reflect on the blessings in life, and focus on the positive rather than the negative. This can lead to a greater sense of contentment and satisfaction with life, even in the face of challenges and difficulties.

Actually, deciding what is ENOUGH is a highly personal and subjective process that requires deep self-reflection and an understanding of one's own values and priorities. It involves setting realistic goals and developing a plan to achieve them, while also making peace with what one already has. By taking the time to determine what is truly important in life and working to achieve it, individuals can find a sense of contentment and fulfilment, no matter what their circumstances may be.

One has to be honest while deciding ENOUGH. To decide what is enough, individuals must first identify their priorities and goals. They must be honest with themselves about what they truly want in life, and what they are willing to do to achieve it. This involves considering factors such as career aspirations, financial stability, relationships, personal values, and spiritual beliefs.

It is important to understand what role Money plays in defining ENOUGH.

Money definitely plays a significant role in defining ENOUGH. It can mean having a certain amount of savings for future social security; being able to afford a sustainable lifestyle and a comfort level.

Careful planning & money management can help an individual be financially free provided he has defined what is going to be ENOUGH for him. Consistent savings for the long term as long as one earns leads to a compounding of money provided invested wisely, one can seek the help of financial advisors if needed. Have you seen those advertisements "Mutual Funds Sahi Hei? Financial freedom can simply mean having enough resources for survival without having to work for earning money.

In another word, financial freedom leads a person to spend time the way he/she wants because he/she does not need to spend time to earn a livelihood. When you spend your time the way you want, it makes you a happier person. Spending your time, the way you want it is one of the most important variables of lifestyle which can be achieved through careful money management.

While money is significant in defining ENOUGH, it is a tool to meet basic needs, the preferred standard of living, goals, ambitions, financial security, social comparisons, influences & duties.

However, it is important to note that it is not the sole determinant. Personal values, relationships, health, and personal growth also contribute to one's overall sense of fulfilment and contentment.

The definition of "ENOUGH" is subjective and can vary greatly from person to person. It is not that one can ask for everything in ENOUGH. They must be honest with themselves about what they truly want as ENOUGH.

So apt is this song from a Bollywood movie Ahista Ahista, sung by Asha Bhosale ji and Bhupinder ji written by Nida Fazli to define ENOUGH. Please listen to it.

Roman English Version -

kabhii kisii ko mukammal jahaan nahiin milataa,

Hindi version-

कभी किसी को मुकम्मल जहाँ नहीं मिलता

कहीं ज़मीन तो कहीं आसमान नहीं मिलता

Gratitude

One day I was perusing through LinkedIn posts. There were a couple of posts about rich and famous people who toiled hard, faced extreme difficulties, but never gave up and achieved success. My mind started to wonder why people only talk about a handful of successes. Just because they are in public life?

As this thought stroked my mind, I started to look around and found so many people that I have met and come across who had their own challenges and worked hard to succeed in their lives. The common point was that all of them defined their expectations as "enough." They worked towards achieving that. One milestone was completed, and the next was set. They never became public figures but are very successful. To mention a few life journeys here:

Be it a young boy from Jalandhar city learning tricks of the trade from his uncle in Delhi and then starting his own distribution from scratch to become a sought-after distributor, his beauty was that he picked up all the good points from his uncle and did not follow his manipulative and wrong tactics.

Be it an area sales manager, moving on to become a distributor with small capital. Working hard to become a known distributor again in Jalandhar city.

Be it a direct sales franchise that started from selling food processors door to door to becoming a big distributor in Lucknow city,

Be it a sales executive in Delhi becoming the president of a large company through sheer hard work, smart work, and developing soft skills

Be it a distributor of Captain Cook salt in Karnal expanding into appliance distribution, becoming a manufacturer of appliances and launching a private label.

So many such success stories fructified in my life, and here was the narrator who told so many stories of ordinary people who faced life's extreme situations, difficulties, and breaking points yet kept on going and achieving their ENOUGH.

At this juncture, the thought came to mind to write down a few of these stories for the benefit of readers, showing them that there is nothing to be sad about in life. Be a hustler.

Actually, there are so many people who have directly and indirectly supported me through my ongoing hustle that acknowledging a few names would not be justified.

However, I wish to thank and acknowledge three people who took care of my health and wealth.

The first person is the late Dr. Pradeep Tara. He was great at knowing how much medication was enough for the patients' cure. Falling sick was no worry with him being there, as we all trusted him. This trust gave me faith, and with faith comes peace. He was taken away by the Delta variant of COVID. Somehow, it felt like I became medically orphaned with his passing.

The second person is Dr. V. S. Madan, the neurosurgeon, who made my serious health issue simpler by generating confidence and treating it without surgery, whereas most of the other doctors had advised it. He always believes in treating the patient, not the MRI or test results. His treatment is determined by the condition of the patient, however bad it may look on an MRI or other test. In my circle, I always recommended him for related issues, and he treated many of them.

The third person is Rohit Raman, M/s Blueant, the finance consultant who helped me create a war chest to be free from the financial worries of daal-roti, aka bread and butter. Blueant is an apt name chosen by Rohit as it symbolises patience, patience, patience! What you are asking for or working towards is coming, but it requires patience and sticking to the path you are currently on. Wealth is created through a compounding effect over a longer period with patience.

I used to tell Rohit that his job was serious since he handled clients' hard-earned money and more precious time. Any error or avarice to increase commissions from funds with low returns might destroy the clients and their future. If the wealth of your clients increases, so will your own. It is the equivalent of a savior.

My elder brother, who really led me to several important life decisions, introduced me to him.

Prior to Rohit, I encountered a couple of CFAs, but they were rather intrusive in their need to understand every aspect of finances and even more information to plan out investments as instructed in their schooling. On the other hand, Rohit never inquired about my salary; instead, he wanted to know how much I could save each month. Of course, he kept motivating me to save more.

By making his customers meet their ENOUGH, Rohit has met his own.

There's still a long journey ahead for all of us. My sincere thanks to all my close friends, mentors, family, and well-wishers who have stood by me and supported me all through my life without seeking any return favors. It is a blessing from God to have such wonderful people in my life. I look forward to the same. They have been more givers than takers, and I too practice being a giver more than what I get and try not to leave any opportunity to extend help.

Stay happy and healthy, Hamesha.

God Bless.

www.ingramcontent.com/pod-product-compliance
Lightning Source LLC
LaVergne TN
LVHW061616070526
838199LV00078B/7298